Samuel French Acting Edition

Paradise Blue

by Dominique Morisseau

SAMUELFRENCH.COM   SAMUELFRENCH.CO.UK

FOR PRODUCTION ENQUIRIES

UNITED STATES AND CANADA
Info@SamuelFrench.com
1-866-598-8449

UNITED KINGDOM AND EUROPE
Plays@SamuelFrench.co.uk
020-7255-4302

Each title is subject to availability from Samuel French, depending upon country of performance. Please be aware that *PARADISE BLUE* may not be licensed by Samuel French in your territory. Professional and amateur producers should contact the nearest Samuel French office or licensing partner to verify availability.

MUSIC USE NOTE

Licensees are solely responsible for obtaining formal written permission from copyright owners to use copyrighted music in the performance of this play and are strongly cautioned to do so. If no such permission is obtained by the licensee, then the licensee must use only original music that the licensee owns and controls. Licensees are solely responsible and liable for all music clearances and shall indemnify the copyright owners of the play(s) and their licensing agent, Samuel French, against any costs, expenses, losses and liabilities arising from the use of music by licensees. Please contact the appropriate music licensing authority in your territory for the rights to any incidental music.

IMPORTANT BILLING AND CREDIT REQUIREMENTS

If you have obtained performance rights to this title, please refer to your licensing agreement for important billing and credit requirements.

PARADISE BLUE received its world premiere at the Williamstown Theatre Festival (Mandy Greenfield, Artistic Director) in Williamstown, Massachusetts on July 22, 2015. The production was directed by Ruben Santiago-Hudson, with sets by Neil Patel, costumes by Clint Ramos, lights by Rui Rita, sound by Darron L West, fights by Thomas Schall, and music co-composed by Kenny Rampton and Bill Sims, Jr. The production stage manager was Lloyd Davis, Jr. The cast was as follows:

PUMPKIN	Kristolyn Lloyd
BLUE	Blair Underwood
CORN	Keith Randolph Smith
P-SAM	André Holland
SILVER	De'Adre Aziza

PARADISE BLUE was produced at Signature Theatre (Paige Evans, Artistic Director; Harold Wolpert, Executive Director) in New York, New York on April 24, 2018. The production was directed by Ruben Santiago-Hudson, with sets by Neil Patel, costumes by Clint Ramos, lights by Rui Rita, sound by Darron L West, fights by Thomas Schall, hair and wigs by Charles G. LaPointe, original music by Kenny Rampton, and music direction by Bill Sims, Jr. The production stage manager was Laura Wilson. The cast was as follows:

PUMPKIN	Kristolyn Lloyd
BLUE	J. Alphonse Nicholson
CORN	Keith Randolph Smith
P-SAM	Francois Battiste
SILVER	Simone Missick

PARADISE BLUE is a recipient of the 2015 Edgerton Foundation New Play Award.

CHARACTERS

PUMPKIN – Black woman, late twenties to early thirties. Pretty in a plain way. Simple, sweet. Waitress, cook and caretaker of Paradise Club. A loving thing with a soft touch. Adores poetry.

BLUE – Black man, mid- to late thirties or early forties. Proprietor of Paradise Club. Handsome, mysterious, sexy. Quietly dangerous. Aloof. A hard shell and a hard interior. Battling many demons. A gifted trumpeter.

CORN (AKA CORNELIUS) – Black man, late forties to early fifties. Slightly chubby. Easygoing and thoughtful, a real sweetheart with a weakness for love. The piano man.

P-SAM (AKA PERCUSSION SAM) – Black man, mid- to late thirties. Busybody, sweet-talker, hustler. Always eager for his next gig. The percussionist.

SILVER – Black woman, late thirties to early forties. Mysterious, sexy, charming. Spicy. Gritty and raw in a way that men find irresistible. Has a meeeeaaaannnn walk.

SETTING

Detroit, Michigan, in a small black community known as Black Bottom, on the downtown strip known as Paradise Valley. Paradise Club.

TIME

1949.

NOTE

A slash (/) indicates where the next line of dialogue begins.

For Pearl Cleage, because of her inspiration to me as a writer. Because of her love of black women in her work. Because of her love of Detroit. And because of her essay, "Mad at Miles" – which gave me the ammunition and bravery to deal with community accountability in and out of my art.

And for the elders who remember a very different Detroit.

peaceandlovedominique ☺

ACT I

Prologue

(In darkness:)

(A trumpet wails a painful tune. It is long and sorrowful, almost a dirge.)

(At rise:)

*(A soft light comes up on **BLUE**. He is silhouetted with his trumpet in hand, the source behind the trumpet's wail. Beads of sweat dance down his face as his notes pierce the air.)*

(The trumpet sings as the tune becomes increasingly beautiful.)

*(Then suddenly, a white light washes over **BLUE**. He plays a long note. It is the most beautiful note we've ever heard.)*

(Finally, he stops, stands there...dripping with sweat. Crying.)

(The white light over him becomes even brighter.)

(He smiles, overcome with peace.)

(A gunshot.)

(Blackout.)

Scene One

(Lights up on an empty nightclub. This is Paradise. A sign in the window that says so is unlit.)

(A cardboard sign in the window says, "Bassist wanted – ask for Blue.")

(A second cardboard sign in the window says, "Rooms upstairs available for rent – ask for Blue.")

(Chairs are mounted on tables. A bar is stage left. Stools are mounted atop. A heap of swept trash sits in the middle of the floor with an abandoned broom nearby.)

*(**PUMPKIN**, a young, pretty, simple woman, enters from the kitchen with a dustpan in one hand and a book of poetry in the other.)*

(She reads with complete engagement, doing an odd job of trying to sweep up the trash without losing her page as she reads.)

PUMPKIN. *(Reciting aloud.)* "The heart of a woman goes forth with the dawn,
As a lone bird, soft winging, so restlessly on,
Afar o'er life's turrets and vales does it roam
In the wake of those echoes the heart calls home."

> *(She carries the dustpan over to the trash can, trying pitifully to balance it all. A trail of trash spills along the way.)*

"The heart of a woman falls back with the night,
And enters some alien cage –"

> *(She notices the trash that she's spilled. She doubles back and sweeps it up, then proceeds to the can again, engulfed in the poetry.)*

"And enters some alien cage in its plight,
And tries to forget it has dreamed of the stars
While it –"

(More trash spills.)

Ah fudge!

(She scoops up the trash, dropping the book.)

(As swear words.) Mother fudge and grits!!!

(She picks up the book. She carefully balances the trash and the book, heads closer to the trash can.)

"And tries to forget it has dreamed of the stars
While it – breaks,

breaks,

breaks

on the sheltering bars."

(Finally, she dumps the trash into the trash can. The book falls in as well.)

Fudge grits and jam!

(She digs into the trash can to retrieve the book. She wipes it free of food and other garbage nasties and flips through the pages.)

My greatest apologies Missus... *(Reads the name on the cover.)* ...Missus Georgia Douglas Johnson. I would never purposefully treat your beautiful words like Paradise Valley trash. No ma'am. Your words don't deserve none of yesterday's apple tart or steak and peas. And certainly it don't deserve none of Corn's peanut shells or Blue's broken whiskey bottles. Your words deserve to be memorized by every waking mind in Black Bottom. Yes, ma'am. Pumpkin's gonna recite your words to whoever needs some...elegance in their day.

(The door to the club opens and **CORNELIUS** *[AKA* **CORN***] enters, followed by* **PERCUSSION**

SAM *[AKA* P-SAM*]*. P-SAM *grabs the cardboard sign from the window.)*

CORN. Hey there Pumpkin. Good morning to ya.

PUMPKIN. Hey there Corn. Hey P-Sam.

P-SAM. Where Blue?

PUMPKIN. Left out this mornin'. Had to go take care of some business downtown, he say. Ya'll hungry? Got some coffee and toast in the back.

CORN. That'd be all right with me.

(P-SAM *holds out the sign.)*

P-SAM. When he put this up?

(PUMPKIN *looks at the sign.)*

PUMPKIN. Don't know. Musta done it just this morning. Wasn't there last night.

P-SAM. You see this, Corn? You know what this mean?

CORN. Mean "Goodbye, Joe."

P-SAM. I told you, Corn. Didn't I tell you? A little tiff. Little tiff my backside. You said it was just a little tiff and now we got to find a new bassist.

CORN. I thought it was little.

P-SAM. Ain't nothin' little when it come to Blue. Didn't I tell you? Soon as he get that bit of anger in him, somethin' little always turn into somethin' jumbo size. I told you.

PUMPKIN. He done fired Joe?

CORN. Blue and Joe got into a little tiff last night –

P-SAM. Little my tailbone.

CORN. Joe wanted more off the top. Wanted Blue to start paying up front, before we play 'steada after.

P-SAM. And what's wrong with that? Ain't nothin' wrong with wanting your money up front –

CORN. But everybody know Blue like it the way Blue like it. Blue been payin' *after* since we been playing together. You don't know cuz you ain't been playin' with him long as me. We been playin' together since he first got this place. I knew his daddy before he left it to him.

P-SAM. That don't mean a hill of beans. If Joe wanna get paid first, ain't nothin' wrong with that.

CORN. Joe don't understand 'bout the way Blue mind work. That's what I'm trying to tell you. Blue don't like nobody questioning his loyalty. Pumpkin know what I'm sayin', don't you, Pumpkin.

PUMPKIN. I know. Blue like things his way cuz that's the only way he understand. Stuff gotta make sense to him. *(Shift.)* I'm gonna go get your coffee and toast.

(**PUMPKIN** *heads into the back.*)

P-SAM. You know as well as I do that Joe was right. Sometimes Blue make you wait all night till he get the money square. By that time the woman you was leavin' with done already left with some other moe. He make you wait on his time all the time and it ain't right. Joe just speakin' his mind...and good for him, Corn. Good for Joe.

CORN. I'm just tellin' ya, Blue got a type of organization to his mind. Joe confusing a lot of that organization. Way Blue see it, waitin' till *after* to pay us make sure we stick around to play. Make it feel like we done earned somethin' by the end of the night. That's the way his daddy taught him. He not seein' the side about it that make you lose your woman to some other cat. That's all Blue see is what he been taught. You just got to understand him, Sam.

P-SAM. I ain't got to understand nothin', Corn. Blue's spot ain't the only jazz spot in town, y'know? This is Paradise Valley. It ain't nothin' but jazz spots all over Black Bottom. And to tell you the truth, they doin' much better for business lately than this spot here.

CORN. This one of the first though. One of the original spots in Black Bottom. Called Paradise 'fore this lil' strip was even called Paradise Valley. Blue like to say – Paradise Valley took its name from him.

P-SAM. See? That's what I'm talkin' about. What kinda sense do that make? Paradise Valley ain't takin' nothin'

from Blue. He think he the original. He ain't nothin'
but everyday ordinary. Same name is a coincidence.
That's all it is.

CORN. This spot was named Paradise first though.

P-SAM. What kinda coffee you be havin' in the mornin',
Corn? What Pumpkin put in that toast you be havin'
every day? Some kinda Blue-don't-do-no-wrong magic
dope or somethin'?

> (**CORN** *laughs.* **PUMPKIN** *enters with a tray of
> food.*)

PUMPKIN. Whipped up some eggs right quick for you too.
Here you go, fellas. Something to start your mornin' off
nice.

> (**CORN** *grabs a plate eagerly.* **P-SAM** *doesn't
> budge.*)

CORN. Thank you kindly, Pumpkin. Sure is nice of you.

PUMPKIN. P-Sam, ain't you hungry? The eggs is scrambled
hard not soft – just like you like 'em.

P-SAM. No thank you, Pumpkin. Whatever Corn's eating,
I'm gonna stay clear of.

CORN. I'll take his.

> (**CORN** *reaches over and scrapes* **P-SAM***'s plate
> onto his.*)

PUMPKIN. Did I do somethin' wrong? I thought you mighta
been hungry. That's why I whipped up some eggs too.

CORN. No Pumpkin, you did just fine. These eggs taste
delicious.

P-SAM. I'm sorry, Pumpkin. I'll take that coffee though.
I just need somethin' to keep me woke up. Blue got us
rehearsing early and he ain't even here.

PUMPKIN. Should be back in a little bit. Just ran downtown
for a sec.

> (*Beat.*)

Hey there Corn, I got a new one for you. Wanna hear
it?

CORN. Love to.

PUMPKIN. You too, P-Sam?

P-SAM. Sure, Pumpkin. We got time to kill. What you got?

PUMPKIN. 'Kay. Almost got it memorized.

> *(Hands **CORN** the book of poems, open to her page.)*

Hold this, Corn. In case I forget.

CORN. All right. Go'on Pumpkin.

PUMPKIN. "The heart of a woman goes forth with the dawn,

As a lone bird, soft winging, so restlessly on..."

Er...ummm...

CORN. Afar?

P-SAM. A who?

PUMPKIN. Oh okay – wait...don't tell me...

"Afar o'er life's turrets and...vales does it roam

In the wake of those echoes the heart calls home."

CORN. That was good there, Pumpkin. Wasn't that good, Sam?

P-SAM. That was good all right. Real smart words you got there, Pumpkin. Make it sound real pretty.

PUMPKIN. They not mine. Miss Georgia Douglas Johnson. They hers.

CORN. What's that part she says here? About "the heart of a woman goes forth with the dawn as a..."

PUMPKIN. Lone bird...

CORN. What's that mean, Pumpkin?

PUMPKIN. I think it means...well...that a woman is just goin' off on her lonesome...waitin' for somebody to love her. Somethin' like that, I think.

P-SAM. Waiting for somebody to love her, hunh Pumpkin?

PUMPKIN. *(Bashfully.)* I think that's what it means...maybe.

CORN. Well I thank you, Pumpkin. For the good words and the good eatin'.

> (**CORN** *slops up the rest of his food.* **P-SAM**
> *watches* **PUMPKIN** *take down chairs from the*
> *tables. He joins her.*)

P-SAM. Lemme help you with these chairs, now.

PUMPKIN. Oh it's all right, P-Sam. I can do it.

P-SAM. You ain't always got to call me P-Sam, you know?

PUMPKIN. I like it better than sayin' Percussion Sam all the way out. P-Sam a good nickname.

P-SAM. Yeah. Sure, Pumpkin. But it's you and me. It's all right if you just call me Sam. That's what anybody close to me call me.

PUMPKIN. I...feel more...proper...callin' you P-Sam.

P-SAM. Proper?

PUMPKIN. For Blue. Don't think he'll like it much, me talkin' to you improper. For a lady.

P-SAM. It ain't Blue's name. You callin' Blue, you call him whatever he say. But when you callin' my name, you can call me Sam.

PUMPKIN. Still...

> (**PUMPKIN** *nervously moseys away from*
> **P-SAM**. *He watches her and smiles.*)

P-SAM. You too sweet, Pumpkin. You got the perfect name for who you is.

> (*The door to the club opens sharply.* **PUMPKIN**
> *jumps and moves over to the bar, wiping it*
> *down profusely.*)

> (**BLUE** *enters. He is a lion of a man, more*
> *in his demeanor than his stature. Thirties*
> *and smooth. He walks in and commands*
> *attention.*)

BLUE. Where the sign go?

CORN. Hey there, Blue.

> (**BLUE** *sees the cardboard sign that* **P-SAM** *had*
> *lying on the counter.*)

BLUE. Who took down the sign?

CORN. We was just lookin' at it. Thought maybe it was a mistake.

BLUE. Ain't no mistake.

CORN. Sam was just lookin' at it.

P-SAM. You fired Joe?

BLUE. Joe quit. I ain't fire nothin'. He quit cuz he's a fool. Good riddance to him.

CORN. Quit? What for?

BLUE. Talkin' 'bout he want some solo time. Everybody know this is Blue's Black Bottom Quartet. My club. My band. Ain't nobody gettin' solo time but me. Don't no bassist nowhere get solo time and he think he just gonna change the rules. Joe a fool. Talkin' 'bout he gonna go'on over to the Three Sixes and get picked up over there. I told him go. Three Sixes ain't better than Paradise Club. I don't care how much money they pullin' in. Money ain't quality.

P-SAM. How we s'pose to play bop without bass? We can't play without Joe.

BLUE. We'll replace Joe. And till we do, I'm goin' on solo. And Corn, I'm puttin' you on too. You gonna do some old standards with Pumpkin for the intermission act.

PUMPKIN. Me?

BLUE. That's right, baby. Just for intermission. You gonna be on the stage and sing for me.

PUMPKIN. But... I –

P-SAM. What's that mean? Pumpkin and Corn doing standards. You doin' solos? Where's that leave me?

BLUE. Leave you with a roof over your head upstairs of my club free of charge. That's what it leave you. 'Less you ready to complain about that now.

P-SAM. How you gonna play solo with no rhythm section? Who's gonna do your rhythm?

BLUE. Got a guest band coming in next Friday. Just gonna play with 'em till we get back swingin'.

P-SAM. Guest band? You bringin' in somebody else to do percussion? What am I supposed to do if I'm not playin'? Sit on empty pockets till the cows come home?

BLUE. Didn't I say it's temporary? You do this till we find somebody to replace Joe. And till then, I ain't gonna charge you no rent. That's fair as I can think to make it. You know somebody else would do you that?

P-SAM. I know somebody else woulda just let Joe have his money up front and we wouldn't be worryin' 'bout none of this. We need to be out there lookin' for a bassist right now. Ain't one just gonna walk in here outta nowhere.

BLUE. Then go'on and look for one. I got other things to take care of right now.

CORN. You been downtown today?

BLUE. That's right. Some folks downtown been comin' 'round here to do some business.

CORN. Safe Eddie say they been comin' 'round by the Echo Theatre and Wilfred's Billiard Parlor too.

P-SAM. Comin' 'round for what? What they comin' 'round for?

CORN. Said they been talkin' about that plan. This new mayor 'bout to take offce – Mayor Cobo...he done ran his campaign on it.

P-SAM. The one where they supposed to be clearin' up the slums?

CORN. Gettin' rid of the *blight* in the city. That's what he say on the radio.

P-SAM. Blight? What's he meanin' by that?

BLUE. He means these run-down buildings over here on Hastings Street. That's what he means. And I don't blame him none. Some of these places are a real eyesore. Make all our spots look run-down. I hope he get rid of it good and send them low-class niggers back to the outskirts of the city so the rest of us can finally move on up.

CORN. Them folks ain't doin' nothin' but living where they can afford. That's all. Ain't they fault some of them buildings is run-down. Half of 'em don't even own them buildings. Just payin' what they can afford. Ain't they fault.

BLUE. Fault don't matter. Long as Black Bottom stay what it is, cramped and overcrowded – we ain't never gonna have what all them white folks got. Niggers always comin' 'round here askin' for handouts and free room and board while they get on they feet. Ain't but so much favors you can do. I rely on these bastards, I'm liable to go bankrupt.

PUMPKIN. I like it here in Black Bottom. Always got somewhere I can count on folks. Know Buffalo James gonna always offer me some of his cornmeal if I run out here. Know Patty Poindexter gonna always give me a press'n'curl whether I got the money to pay her or gotta owe it to her the next time. These folks over here like family. Always got time to pull favors for family.

BLUE. Ain't nobody pullin' no more favors outta me. I been pullin' favors up to my ears and I'm goin' tone-deaf.

CORN. What was they tellin' you Blue? Them folks downtown?

BLUE. Just come askin' about Paradise. Say the land this club is sittin' on is pretty hot. More footage than the other spots around here. City wants a piece. Maybe offerin' me a pretty penny for it.

PUMPKIN. You gonna sell Paradise?

BLUE. I ain't sayin' all that. I just say they come talkin' 'bout it. So I go hear what they got to say. That's all.

P-SAM. Ain't this somethin? First you fire Joe and now you gon' put all us on the street if them downtown fellas talk to you right!

BLUE. Didn't I say I was hearin' what they got to say? Don't be puttin' words in my mouth, you hear me? And I done already told you – Joe quit!

P-SAM. Cuz you makin' him quit!

BLUE. If you don't like it, nigger, then there go the door. Ain't nobody askin' you to stay 'round here.

P-SAM. I just might, Blue. Don't go sayin' nothin' just to say it. I just might.

CORN. Ain't no need for all that. Percussion Sam and Corn the Piano Man both a part of Blue's Black Bottom Quartet and we know that, Blue. Ain't no need for nobody else to quit. We gonna find a bassist and be back in business. And till then, you go 'head and work on your solo while me and Pumpkin learn ourselves some standards.

PUMPKIN. But... I don't think –

BLUE. Sheet music's upstairs. I'll get it and ya'll can practice in back while I get this spot ready for dinner tonight. Ya'll learn it and be ready to go up by next Friday. And in the meantime, Sam can go'on and find us a bassist at Garfield's Lounge he wanna be so ambitious.

P-SAM. You ain't sayin' nothin' but a word.

BLUE. All right then.

> *(The door to the club opens. A mysterious-looking woman dressed in black enters. She wears a hat and veil. This is* **SILVER**.*)*

> *(Everyone stops and looks at her. She moves like a spider weaving a web. They watch her until she stops.)*

SILVER. Is Blue here?

> *(Everyone looks at* **BLUE**. *He looks at* **SILVER** *questioningly.)*

BLUE. I'm Blue. I know you, lady?

SILVER. Naw. But your sign in the window say you got rooms for rent. That true?

BLUE. Oh...yeah...yeah that's true. I got one-person rooms for rent. Not enough space for your ol' man or nothin'. Them kinda rooms is already occupied.

SILVER. My ol' man dead. How much you charge for your rooms?

BLUE. Five dollars a week. That include meals.

SILVER. Five dollars a week? That ain't comparable. Place up the street got rooms for three dollars a week.

BLUE. Place up the street ain't got nice hot water every day for you neither. Go'on ask folks – you think I'm lying. Lay down for a nice sleep and wake up to a roach openin' your blinds and askin' you how you like yo' grits.

SILVER. Your rooms clean?

BLUE. Pristine. Pumpkin see to that.

SILVER. Pumpkin?

> (**PUMPKIN** *stares at* **SILVER** *in awe...and suddenly snaps out of it.*)

PUMPKIN. Oh yes, Missus. I keep it nice and tidy for you and I starch your sheets clean. If you need anything, you can always let me know and I'll see to it for you.

BLUE. Place up the street ain't got that for you. But you go'on stay up there if you think they better than what we got over here.

SILVER. And what about playin' that bop? You keep late hours?

BLUE. We keep as late hours as any of these other clubs in Paradise Valley. You in Black Bottom, Detroit. And this lil' strip is what we call the jazz paradise. You don't like bop or blues, you got a long way to go 'fore you find some place without it.

SILVER. I ain't said I ain't like it. I know where I'm at. *(Pause.)* What if I wanna stay longer than a week?

BLUE. Long as you can pay, you can stay.

SILVER. Well then...

> (**SILVER** *digs into her bosom and pulls out a wad of cash. Everyone watches her in astonishment. She hands money to* **BLUE**.)

That's thirty dollars. I want the month and then some...

> (**BLUE** *counts the cash twice over...eyeing it widely.*)

BLUE. Go'on with her, Pumpkin. Show this woman where the room at.

PUMPKIN. All right then...you can follow me, Missus...You got a name?

SILVER. They call me Silver.

PUMPKIN. Silver? Well all right, follow me, Miss Silver.

(**SILVER** *follows* **PUMPKIN** *out.*)

(**P-SAM** *and* **CORN** *look after them.*)

P-SAM. Whooo!!! You see that woman?

CORN. Seen her, I did.

P-SAM. She got some kinda walk on her, ain't she?

BLUE. She got some kinda money on her. You see her pull this out that fast? Somethin' ain't right about that.

CORN. What ain't right about it? She look right to me.

BLUE. What a woman doin' comin' here with no ol' man? You hear that? Talkin' 'bout, "My ol' man dead." Say it just like that, without no feelin' or nothin'. Somethin' ain't right about it.

P-SAM. She ain't got no man and she got a walk like that, she ain't gonna be in that one-person room too long.

CORN. She got some kinda sadness to her maybe.

BLUE. Whatever she is, she better not bring no trouble up here in Paradise. Woman like that...lookin' the way she lookin'...all on her lonesome...them kinda women ain't nothin' but trouble. You betta believe that.

P-SAM. Well a little bit of trouble ain't never hurt nobody really. *(Shift.)* I'm gon' get on. Since we ain't rehearsing no more, I'ma go try my luck with the policy. Maybe if I bet just right, my number'll come up and I won't have to worry 'bout having no gig right now. Hmph... Joe quit...

(**P-SAM** *heads on out the door.*)

BLUE. Corn, that nigger gonna try me. I'm tellin' you. That P-Sam ain't worth the trust I'd give a honkie on a Tuesday.

CORN. He all right, Blue. We gonna find us somebody that's gonna turn things around here. You'll see.

BLUE. Yeah, I'll see. *(Shift.)* Gonna get you that sheet music for Pumpkin. You got to help her sing it right.

CORN. All right, Blue. If that's what you need.

BLUE. That's what I need, Corn. She be scared and nervous... but you help her. I hear her humming and singing soft, and it sound real pretty. She got a voice in her. But you got to help it come out. You the only one can ease it out of her. You get me?

CORN. Yeah I get you, Blue.

BLUE. Good, Corn. That's good.

(**BLUE** *exits.*)

CORN. *(Softly.)* I may be the only one who do get you...

(Lights shift.)

Scene Two

(SILVER's room. It's rather plain, just a twin bed, a small vanity, one tall dresser. Maybe a broken-framed hanging picture. That's all, folks. PUMPKIN makes the bed while SILVER unpacks.)

PUMPKIN. ...and the meals regular – breakfast, lunch and dinner. So you just gotta let me know if you eatin' every night or if you gettin' your meal somewhere else. Best meal is supper. I'm usually 'lowed to give three sides 'steada two. So I switch it up. Corn hash with roast beef and string beans, cabbage, and cranberry sauce...or sometimes we do steak and peas with mashed potato and gravy – Blue count gravy as a side on that one – and on Fridays we usually do the fish fry with some kinda potato and greens. We got hot sauce packets but we charge a penny if you want more than two. And –

(SILVER stares at PUMPKIN.)

What'sthematter? Am I talkin' your ear off? Blue say I could talk a hole in your head if don't nobody tell me to hush.

SILVER. You do the cookin'?

PUMPKIN. Yes, Missus. I'm a real good cook.

SILVER. Umph. I hate cookin'.

PUMPKIN. Do you?

SILVER. With a passion. Can't stand the heat of nobody else's kitchen. I prefer the heat in the bedroom or some other places. But not in the kitchen. That's the wrong kinda heat for me.

PUMPKIN. Oh. *(Short pause.)* Well it's good I'll do it for you then. No worries there.

(SILVER pulls out a record player and sets it atop the dresser. She pulls out a couple of records.)

My goodness. You travel with that thing?

SILVER. Can't be one place and my music someplace else. Go crazy otherwise...

> (SILVER *pulls out a silky nightgown and holds it up to herself in the mirror.* PUMPKIN *watches in astonishment.*)

This thing...ain't worth the rocks in my shoes. Silk my tailbone. This some kinda imposter fabric if I ever seen it. I knew that man sold it to me was lyin', but the store lights wasn't harsh as these. I can see real good now. Cheap rayon maybe. Not no silk.

PUMPKIN. I think it's pretty.

SILVER. It's yours then.

> (SILVER *tosses it to* PUMPKIN *nonchalantly and continues to unpack her clothes.*)

PUMPKIN. Oh! No – Missus I couldn't –

SILVER. Sho you can.

PUMPKIN. But it's yours.

SILVER. Not no more. Don't like the thing.

PUMPKIN. But, I –

SILVER. So which one of them fellas your ol' man?

PUMPKIN. Oh – well, me and Blue are together –

SILVER. 'Course you are. He the one who runnin' everything. *(Shift.)* So them other two fellas...they up for grabs then?

PUMPKIN. Well I...they are... I mean... I wouldn't know...

SILVER. That mean they are. If they wasn't, you would know. Believe me that.

PUMPKIN. What brings you over here to Black Bottom?

SILVER. Time to pick up somewhere new. I heard of Black Bottom, Detroit. 'Specially down this strip in Paradise Valley where folks got all they own business. If it's somewhere that colored folks is doing more than sharecroppin' and reapin' white folks' harvest... I ought to be there. They say that here's where folks sellin' automobiles and bettin' on the policy numbers and dancin' in the nighttime like they just as free as the Mississippi River. I'm here so I can get a taste of all that.

PUMPKIN. Where you come from?

SILVER. Lots of places. But Louisiana be the first.

PUMPKIN. Louisiana? Place where they got all them spirits and Negroes eatin' live chickens and drinkin' they blood?

*(**SILVER** looks at **PUMPKIN** questioningly.)*

SILVER. You ain't never been, have you?

PUMPKIN. No, miss. Never been outside Detroit.

SILVER. Well, maybe you oughta leave sometime. And when you do, try out Louisiana.

PUMPKIN. I love it here in Black Bottom. I don't never wanna leave.

SILVER. That so? Why's that?

PUMPKIN. Got roots here. And purpose.

SILVER. Got family here?

PUMPKIN. Made family here. Was sent here as a girl to stay with my aunt who run her own beauty parlor on Hastings Street. Used to work for her and attend school over there. She passed on now, and the parlor been turned into an automobile store. But I stayed around here. With different women what used to be her customers. They took care of me. Even helped to pay for my books. And eventually I met Blue.

SILVER. And the rest was history, hunh?

PUMPKIN. Yes, ma'am.

SILVER. Well, it's good you made you some roots here, but every woman got to pick up and leave after while. If you don't know that now, you gonna know it one day.

PUMPKIN. *(Remembering.)* "The heart of a woman goes forth with the dawn..."

SILVER. What's that?

PUMPKIN. A little bit of poetry. Just made me think of it.

SILVER. You a poet? Like them fellas in Harlem?

PUMPKIN. No, not me. I just like it, that's all. What you said about a woman pickin' up and leavin'...remind me of some poetry. It say – "The heart of a woman goes forth with the dawn..." I suppose that's what you doin'.

SILVER. Well, that's fancy of you. Recitin' poems like that from your memory. Maybe that's somethin' you can learn me how to do.

PUMPKIN. Oh. *(Bashful smile.)* Sure...

> *(**SILVER** finishes putting her clothes away. She takes off her shirt and bottoms nonchalantly – leaving her in striking undergarments. She sprays herself with perfume. **PUMPKIN** stares at her, fascinated.)*

SILVER. This fella of yours...he be good to you?

PUMPKIN. Blue. He's something special. Gifted.

SILVER. That wasn't my question.

PUMPKIN. I'm sorry?

SILVER. I say, he be good to you? That's important to ask a woman 'bout a man. I done learned.

PUMPKIN. He the best thing I've ever known.

SILVER. That so?

PUMPKIN. Yes, Missus. Got a gentle heart and a lion's soul. Got the will to give me everything he can. But what he really got is a gift. It make it so sometimes that's all I can see. When he play, I think he's talkin' to God and together they answerin' my prayers.

SILVER. Weelll...he must do you real good – up, down and inside...way you speak on him like ecstasy.

PUMPKIN. My goodness. You always speak this improper?

SILVER. What's improper 'bout it? I'm just speakin' straight. Ain't that what these Detroit gangsters do? Speak straight.

PUMPKIN. Why a woman need to speak like a gangster?

SILVER. *(Seriously.)* So everybody know she ain't to be messed with.

> *(Beat.)*

I can get me one of them nice hot suppers you was talkin' 'bout this evening?

PUMPKIN. Oh...yes, Missus. 'Round eight o'clock. I'll be by to deliver it to you.

SILVER. That's fine by me. Now if you don't mind, I got to finish messin' with my things and get into somethin' comfortable.

PUMPKIN. Oh – right.

>(**PUMPKIN** *moves to the door with a touch of embarrassment.*)

If you need anything else, you just ring me and I'll take care of you. Phone booth is in the hallway out there. But I'm usually downstairs.

SILVER. Be sure to.

>(**PUMPKIN** *opens the door.*)

And don't forget this. It's yours now.

>(**SILVER** *throws* **PUMPKIN** *the nightgown.*)

>(**PUMPKIN** *– clueless of what to do – nods and disappears behind the door.*)

>(**SILVER** *watches after her for a moment... calculatingly.*)

>(*Then she sits down at the vanity and dolls herself up for the night.*)

Scene Three

(Afternoon sun spills through Paradise Club.
CORN *sits at the bar and demolishes a hearty meal.)*

*(***PUMPKIN*** *wipes down the bar and fills the liquor stock. Occasionally, she winces from a pain in her wrist. No one notices.)*

CORN. Pumpkin, you put your foot in this cornbread.

PUMPKIN. Not supposed to give it to you till supper, but I thought maybe you could have a light taste. For listenin' to my poetry and all...

CORN. You keep fillin' me up with this stuff, I listen to a hundred of your poems. Hit me.

*(***PUMPKIN*** *eagerly rushes to the bar and picks up a book. She passes it to* ***CORN***.*)

PUMPKIN. This one she calls, "My Little Dreams."

CORN. She who?

PUMPKIN. Miss Georgia Douglas Johnson. My latest favorite. Goes like this...

"I'm folding up my little dreams

Within my heart tonight,

And praying I may soon forget

The torture of their sight.

For time's deft fingers scroll my brow

With fell relentless art –

I'm folding up my little dreams

Tonight, within my heart."

CORN. What kind of fingers is that, Pumpkin? Say it scroll on the brow?

PUMPKIN. Deft. Means like, you know, how somebody got good knittin' hands? Fingers got lots of skill. That's what time got. Deft fingers. And you ever known how somebody rubbin' on your head, say a woman maybe? And she maybe smooth your eyebrow some...

CORN. I ain't know that in a long time. Not since my Mabel passed.

PUMPKIN. Well, that's what Miss Johnson means in her poetry. Time massaging her like your Mabel used to do you. Movin' on till it's gone and her dreams gone too. She bury them in her heart so she don't have to think on 'em or be sad no more. Like your Mabel.

CORN. Yeah. I buried her all right. I know what that Miss Johnson mean. Bury something deep inside so you can forget the hurt of not havin' it.

PUMPKIN. That's right, Corn. That's real good. You're a regular poet. An interpreter. That's what you are.

CORN. Naw, Pumpkin. That's you and this stuff. I just like to listen with you cuz it's somethin' different. We got the piano. Got the trumpet. Got the percussion. Used to have the bass. Then you come with these words and bring in another kind of music.

> *(The door to the club swings open. In walks*
> **P-SAM**.*)*

P-SAM. Hey there, folks.

CORN. Hey, Sam.

PUMPKIN. Afternoon, P-Sam.

P-SAM. *(Flirtatious.)* Hey, Pumpkin pie. Got a little somethin' for me to nibble on?

PUMPKIN. Today we got sandwiches for lunch. Bologna and salami. I'll go make you one.

P-SAM. What's that Corn was eating over here? That don't look like no crumbs from a sandwich.

CORN. Yes it was, wasn't it, Pumpkin? Sandwich with the works.

> *(***PUMPKIN*** giggles.)*

P-SAM. Oh I get it. Ain't that nothin'? Corn get to taste an early dinner and all I get is a measly ol' salami sandwich.

PUMPKIN. I'll go put you some pickles on it too...

P-SAM. Well la-ti-da. I guess I'm s'pose to jump out my shoes cuz I get pickles.

(**PUMPKIN** *disappears into the back.*)

Say, Corn, I found us somebody.

CORN. Did you?

P-SAM. String-Finger Charlie over at Garfield's Lounge. Caught his set last night and it's outta sight. Talked to him – say he lookin' to leave Percy's quintet if Blue willin' to meet his fee. Percy payin' them overtime if the set runs late.

CORN. Don't know if Blue gonna go for that now, Sam. You know he don't believe in overtime.

P-SAM. Blue don't believe in nothin' but himself. Where I'm s'pose to play, Corn? Ain't no openings for a percussion man at none of these other clubs in the valley.

CORN. You a good musician, Sam. You can get your pick anywhere.

P-SAM. Don't give me that, Corn. Ain't no place for a colored man outside of Black Bottom and you know it. I been on that other stint, playin' the white man's club in Detroit and all them other cities – entering through the back door. Carryin' my card in Harlem and if I ain't got it, I ain't allowed to make no bread or play no music. Standin' on them stages and smilin' like I'm just happy to be entertainin' these no-'count crackers that think of me as less than the spilled whiskey on they shoe.

CORN. We all been on that stint Sam. One time or another. That's the cost we pay to play.

P-SAM. Tell you the truth, Corn, Blue ain't no better. He think of us just like they do. On the bottom. Only difference is he still a nigger himself, whether he like it or not, and stingy as he is, he need us. And we need each other. That's why we got to get back in business. This the only place I can be a percussion man befo' bein' colored. You the only one can talk to Blue, Corn.

CORN. I don't know String-Finger Charlie. How good is he?

P-SAM. Seen 'im last night do this thing ain't never seen a bassman do befo'. Tap on the strings like a hammer and make two strings play by themselves. Tellin' you – this cat's outta sight.

CORN. Maybe I'll go over to Garfield's Lounge with you tonight and see for myself.

P-SAM. You do that, Corn. And then you talk to Blue. I can't be sittin' here with no money swellin' my pockets. When a Negro man ain't got no money, it's like he smell different. Negro women sniff him miles away and turn they noses in another direction. Not even the finest cologne can clean up that kinda stink. And I'm funky, Corn. It ain't right.

CORN. I'll see. That's all I can say.

P-SAM. That's all you need to say for now. *(Shift.)* How that rehearsin' with Pumpkin goin'?

> (**CORN** *looks back to see if* **PUMPKIN** *is near. Coast is clear.)*

CORN. Terrible.

P-SAM. She that bad?

CORN. Worse.

P-SAM. Well I guess you can't have it all. Be all smart on them books, and sing like you know the devil up close and personal.

CORN. I don't know what to tell Blue 'bout it. He say he done heard her sing pretty but I ain't heard it yet. Ain't got the heart to make her feel bad. But she workin' and workin' and sound like she gettin' worser and worser.

P-SAM. Well serve Blue right, then. Put her up there and see what kinda mess it is, and then maybe he'll see the light.

CORN. I hope he see befo' Friday. He say she got a voice in her somewhere. But I can't find it nowhere.

> *(The door to Paradise Club swings open.* **BLUE** *walks in carrying his trumpet. Zoot suit and hat, lookin' sharp.)*

Afternoon, Blue. You lookin' like Sunday on a Tuesday. Where you comin' from?

BLUE. Just out takin' care of business. Where Pumpkin?

CORN. In the back fixin' P-Sam a sandwich.

BLUE. *(To* **P-SAM.***)* You pay her?

P-SAM. I thought I was gettin' room and board free till we get more gigs?

BLUE. Board ain't meals.

P-SAM. What's board if it ain't meals?! Include meals for everybody else.

BLUE. Everybody else payin'. I'm lettin' you stay up there for free. Don't mean I can afford to feed you with no money. You ain't suckin' me dry.

P-SAM. How I'm supposed to bring in money when you runnin' off musicians every chance you get?

BLUE. Don't start with me on that, nigger. I ain't startin' in with you today.

P-SAM. Listen to that. You hear that, Corn? He ain't startin' in with me. But he the one startin' everything.

*(***PUMPKIN** *enters with the sandwich.)*

PUMPKIN. Here ya go, P-Sam. I made it with pickles and hot sauce too.

BLUE. You charge him the penny for the hot sauce?

PUMPKIN. Well...no...not this time. We had a little extra so –

BLUE. We done been through this, Pumpkin...you can't keep passin' out favors like this is some kinda soup kitchen.

P-SAM. You go'on, Pumpkin. You keep that sandwich, hear? I ain't got to eat nothin' from this penny-pinchin' pistol.

PUMPKIN. Blue, sweets, if he don't eat it, it's just gonna go to waste. Might as well not let no food hit the trash. Ain't that what you told me?

BLUE. Give him the sandwich. But you got to pay sometime. This ain't no soup kitchen. You give niggers one and they want two. Tell 'em free room and they want free meals too.

P-SAM. Sam don't need nothin' for free, hear?

PUMPKIN. Here you go, P-Sam. Eat up. I made it real fine. Gonna go back and get you somethin' to wash it down with too.

> (**PUMPKIN** *exits into the kitchen.* **P-SAM** *picks up his sandwich and bites into it rebelliously.*)

P-SAM. Sam willin' to work for everything he got. Don't need no handouts. But you got me over here without no gig –

BLUE. Thought you was takin' care of that.

P-SAM. I am. Ain't that right, Corn?

CORN. That's right. We gonna go tonight to check out somebody s'posed to be real good.

BLUE. How that song comin' with you and Pumpkin?

CORN. Oh it's...goin'...special. Pumpkin's voice is... somethin' I can't even...explain...

BLUE. Good. You just gotta get her to some confidence. I can hear the music in her speak. You just gotta push it out of her. Woman like Pumpkin need a little push...

CORN. We gonna...push...much as we can...

BLUE. That bad-luck woman been down here today?

CORN. That fiiine woman.

P-SAM. Make you wanna follow wherever she lead...

BLUE. Don't go followin' her 'less you wanna end up in a grave somewhere.

CORN. What you talkin' now, Blue?

BLUE. She already the talk of the town and ain't been here three days.

CORN. What they sayin'?

BLUE. Just what I was thinkin'. Woman move up here without no man got trouble followin' her. Sittin' on a stack of money. Say she killed a man for it.

CORN. Killed a man?

P-SAM. I ain't heard that. But Jimmy the Greek Johnson over at the pool hall was sayin' she done slept with over fifty men in different cities and they all disappeared.

CORN. You listenin' to Jimmy the Greek? You know he ain't never told a truth in his natural life.

BLUE. This time I believe it. I'm tellin' you. I don't trust that woman.

P-SAM. What woman do you trust?

BLUE. Don't start in on me, nigger.

P-SAM. Say they call her a witch.

CORN. Witch?

BLUE. A voodoo woman from Louisiana. That's what she is.

P-SAM. Spiderwoman. That's what they call her. Say she been to Chicago and Minneapolis and Milwaukee too. All them places, she go walkin' like that...some kinda sexy spider...lurin' fellas into her web. And then just when you get close to her...she stick into you and lay her poison.

CORN. *(Laughing.)* If ya'll don't sound like two of the silliest cats to ever play bop...

BLUE. You laugh if you want to, Corn...but you be the first one to get caught up in her web. Then you touch her one time and your longleg fall right off. Them Louisiana women got them spirits in them.

> *(**SILVER** enters from the kitchen, unbeknownst to the men.)*

P-SAM. You got to admit you curious about a lil' of it. But I like my longleg too much to take a bet on that. I rather try my luck with the policy.

SILVER. Afternoon, fellas.

> *(The men jump. **SILVER** smiles a sexy, sinful smile. She spider-walks over to the bar and takes a seat.)*

Hope I'm not interruptin' your man talk. But I was promised me a taste of early dinner and I want to cash in.

BLUE. We got sandwiches. Pumpkin be back out and take care of you.

SILVER. I look like the kind of woman eat sandwiches?

BLUE. *(Glares at* **SILVER.***)* That's what you eatin' / you eatin' here.

SILVER. *(To* **CORN.***)* Say there, buttercup. You got a light?

CORN. Me?

SILVER. I don't see nobody else cute and chubby sittin' over here.

CORN. *(Smiling.)* Well... I don't smoke none.

   *(***BLUE** *slides her some matches.)*

SILVER. Thanks, doll.

   *(***SILVER** *lights a cigarette and takes a slow drag. The men watch her silently.)*

You ought to have yourself a lighter. Every business owner got one of them. Personalized and inscripted. You ought to have that.

BLUE. I got what I need.

SILVER. That's what everybody think...till what they really need come along... *(Shift.)* You fellas read the paper?

BLUE. You want the paper, you got to go'on over to Biddy's restaurant and spend your penny like everybody else. That don't come with the board.

SILVER. Oh, I got my paper for the day. Been doin' my reading too. See what this new mayor of yours got plannin' for this Black Bottom area. Tryin' to clean it up, I see.

P-SAM. That's right, ma'am. They lookin' for folks like us to get on outta here so they can hurry up and make Detroit bright white. But we ain't goin' nowhere...so you don't worry your pretty lil' self 'bout that.

SILVER. Well I just figures...when a city want folks to leave, they must be offerin' somethin' pretty to get rid of 'em. And you especially, sittin' on the ripest piece of somethin' over here. Say the square footage of your land bigger 'n all the other spots in this whole valley. This spot dead in the middle and in the best location.

BLUE. What of it?

SILVER. I just wonder what they offerin' for a place as hot as this.

BLUE. What's it matter to you?

SILVER. Don't matter nothin' yet. Could matter a whole lot if you was interested in sellin'.

BLUE. You think I'm gonna sell my place?

CORN. Blue ain't partin' with this club. This used to be his daddy's club.

BLUE. Leave my daddy outta this, Corn. Miss, you can keep your sidesteppin' slick talk cuz it ain't shakin' over here. Paradise Club is mine, and I ain't talkin' 'bout my plans with no simple woman.

SILVER. Cool down, sugar. I'm just makin' small talk.

BLUE. Ain't nothin' to talk about. Stuff you hearin' 'bout Paradise Club ain't nothin' but hearsay. Niggers runnin' off at the mouth cuz they ain't got nothin' better to do than worry 'bout Blue. But it ain't none of nobody's business what I do with my own spot.

SILVER. Sho, it is. What you do with yo' spot might be real influential to all others. Seem like what you do be everybody business. So you let me know if there's anything worth talkin' 'bout.

BLUE. You think you know somethin' I don't?

SILVER. I know 'bout how to run a club.

P-SAM. Where you know all that?

SILVER. Come from music. My daddy was a bluesman. Grew up 'round all this type of business. And I could tell you why that Garfield's Lounge and the Three Sixes gonna keep having way more customers than over here...even though you got the bigger joint.

P-SAM. Why's that?

CORN. Sam –

SILVER. Chargin' too much at the door.

BLUE. I charge what I charge.

P-SAM. What you think it oughta be?

SILVER. Should only be fifty cents. But you makin' it a whole seventy-five. Too high. Folks see that and don't care that you got the better trumpeteer or the best pecan pie. They feel like they bein' kept on the outskirts. All the other spots make 'em feel welcome. But here, it feel like everybody don't belong. Like even if we all the same people, only certain kinds get to come in and patron. You dividin' the people like pie. That's what make it not feel right.

BLUE. I ain't askin' for your business help. I been runnin' this place for five years just fine.

SILVER. Five years ain't nothin'. I seen goldfish last longer than five years. Five years still wet behind the ears if you ask –

> (**BLUE** *bangs his hand on the bar. Everyone jumps a bit.*)

CORN. Blue.

BLUE. *(Threateningly.)* Watch your mouth in my spot, woman.

CORN. Hey now, Blue –

> (**BLUE** *walks closer to* **SILVER**.)

BLUE. Don't you think you 'bout to come in here and tell me how to run my place. You ain't been in this town five seconds and you think you know 'bout over here in Black Bottom?

> (**SILVER** *remains calm. She smiles and puffs her cigarette.*)

SILVER. I just thought you'd like to hear another idea, sugar. No need to get so uptight.

BLUE. You listen to me here. You come down here, you keep your mouth shut unless you wanna be out of a room. Don't think just cuz you got a stash somewhere that make you matter over here. It don't. I'll throw this money back in your face, put you out on your simple black ass, and won't think twice about it. You understand me, woman?

(**PUMPKIN** *enters from the kitchen.*)

PUMPKIN. Everything all right out here? Blue, sweets, you okay?

(**BLUE** *moves away from* **SILVER** *and grabs his hat.*)

BLUE. Pumpkin, come on and let's get you somethin' to wear for Friday night. Gotta find you somethin' classy for when you sing with Corn.

PUMPKIN. *(Hesitantly.)* But don't you want me to...finish gettin' dinner together for this evenin'? And I still gotta mop the kitchen and change the sheets upstairs –

BLUE. Forget about all that right now. We'll take care of that later. Just grab your coat and meet me in the back. We take the streetcar on down to J. L. Hudson's and pick you out something nice.

PUMPKIN. J. L. Hudson's? We goin' down Woodward?!

BLUE. That's right. For my woman – only the biggest and the fanciest department store in the city. Grab your coat and come on.

P-SAM. J. L. Hudson's? They only 'low niggers to clean they floors and run they elevators. What kinda nigger you think you is to go shoppin' there?

BLUE. They don't let niggers like you shop there. I ain't you.

PUMPKIN. Oh, Blue! You think we can afford it?

BLUE. Don't worry 'bout what we can afford, woman! Just come on and let me get you somethin'.

(**PUMPKIN** *rushes over to grab her coat from the rack. She lifts it and a pain stabs her wrist. She finches.* **SILVER** *notices, as does* **CORN**.)

CORN. You all right there, Pumpkin?

PUMPKIN. Oh, I'm just fine. Little soreness of my wrists. Get that way sometimes when I been cleanin' a lot. Just need to soak 'em in some salts and I be fine.

SILVER. Get you a box a raisins and a pint of gin.

P-SAM. Say what?

SILVER. Louisiana remedy. My grandmama taught it to me. Soak the raisins in a half pint of gin and watch all the pain go away.

P-SAM. What's the other half-pint of gin for?

SILVER. In case of anything else you need to cure. Gin make all kinda pain disappear...

BLUE. Pumpkin don't need none of your backwater Louisiana hoodoo. She'll be just fine.

> (**BLUE** *moves to* **PUMPKIN**'s *side and helps her into her coat.*)

When we get back, Corn, ya'll get back to practicin'.

CORN. Sure, Blue. Whatever you say...

> (**BLUE** *and* **PUMPKIN** *exit.*)

P-SAM. Say, Corn, we should head over to Garfield's 'round eight to see my man String-Finger Charlie.

CORN. I'll be ready.

SILVER. Heard they serving a sweet potato pie over at that lounge tonight that taste better than your Aunt Harriet's.

P-SAM. You want to come have a taste, baby?

SILVER. That's all right, sugar. I was plannin' on stayin' to my lonesome this evening.

P-SAM. Suit yourself, sweetheart. I'm gon' go put my bet in for the policy. You got a favorite number, baby? Maybe I'll play it for you.

SILVER. One three one.

P-SAM. One three one? How you gonna tell me something like that? One three one? You tryin' to curse me?

> (**P-SAM** *heads for the door, disgruntled.*)

I'll see you later, Corn. *(Mumbling.)* One three one... crazy woman...

> (**SILVER** *turns to* **CORN** *and smiles.*)

SILVER. What's got him so uptight?

CORN. You just gave him a number with thirteen in it. Nobody plays thirteen. It's an omen.

SILVER. Oh... I just gave him my old address. One three one Rue Decatur in N'awlins. Men 'round here just act so fussy 'bout every little thang.

CORN. That's just the way these fellas are. Don't pay them no nevermind, miss. I think you were mighty nice – offerin' up your address to him like that. Let him find his own good luck.

> (**SILVER** *smiles at* **CORN**. *She rises from her seat.*)

SILVER. Say there, buttercup... You're a real sweet fella. I can see that from here.

CORN. Thank you, miss. Name's Cornelius. But I like Buttercup just the same.

SILVER. Well, you can call me whatever you like.

> *(She heads for the door.)*

Enjoy that sweet potato pie tonight. And if it's as good as they say, you let me know, will ya?

CORN. I surely will.

> (**SILVER** *winks at* **CORN**, *does her spider-walk, and exits.* **CORN** *sits and smiles after her.*)

Scene Four

(Nighttime falls on the club. Moonlight peeks through the window.)

*(In silhouette, **BLUE** plays his trumpet. He plays a beautiful and painful melody – long, sorrowful notes.)*

*(Soft lights illuminate the rest of the club and reveal **PUMPKIN** putting up chairs. Somewhere in his tune, she leaves one chair down near the foot of the stage, and takes a seat, listening.)*

*(**BLUE** – in his own world – becomes too wrapped up in his pain. Suddenly he breaks free of the tune.)*

(He stops and wipes his face...from sweat...or tears...or both...)

*(**PUMPKIN** applauds.)*

PUMPKIN. That sounded real good.

BLUE. Don't clap for that. Don't ever clap for that.

PUMPKIN. But...it was good.

BLUE. Mediocre. I lost my rhythm. Let it take over. Ain't never s'pose to let it take over.

PUMPKIN. That ain't nothin' but the pain swoopin' in on you. That's what makes it the most beautiful, I think. The pain is the sweetest part.

BLUE. It's weak. Need to practice more 'steada runnin' 'round this city chasin' pipe dreams.

PUMPKIN. Come 'ere.

> *(**BLUE** looks at **PUMPKIN**. For the first time, we see him soften to her. For this one moment, she is in command.)*
>
> *(He walks over to her and kneels beside her. He grabs her waist and holds on to her.)*

You look tired.

BLUE. I am tired, Pumpkin.

PUMPKIN. You can rest now.

BLUE. Ain't no rest for the weary...ain't that how it go?

PUMPKIN. You can rest here. With me.

BLUE. This is dead, Pumpkin.

PUMPKIN. What's dead?

BLUE. This place. Black Bottom. I'm chokin' here. I can hear it when I play my axe. Baby, I'm not right.

PUMPKIN. You sound all right to me. Just achin' inside. But ain't nothin' wrong with that. Everybody got aches. Just need somethin' soft to touch it and make it better. I can do that...if you let me.

BLUE. They're still here, Pumpkin. Them spirits.

PUMPKIN. What spirits?

BLUE. Spirit of my daddy. Lurkin' 'round this club. Hangin' in the walls. Hangin' in my music. Nigger won't leave me be.

PUMPKIN. Those just bad memories. You keep playing till it don't hurt no more.

BLUE. They more than memories, Pumpkin. They my daddy's demons comin' after me. I got to run from 'em 'fore they kill me.

PUMPKIN. Run where, Blue? What you sayin'?

BLUE. I'm gettin' rid of this place, Pumpkin. Gonna sell it to the city. They offerin' ten thousand for this club. That's what I been doin'. Talkin' them into givin' me what I ask for.

PUMPKIN. Sell Paradise?!

BLUE. And go to Chicago. I got these fellas comin' Friday. They got a band in Chicago and they want a trumpet man. I told 'em to come hear me play so they can see I'm the one. Say they lookin' for a songbird to sing with the band sometimes. I told 'em I got the prettiest little songbird in Detroit with me. So you show 'em your pipes and get 'em to understand, Pumpkin. Get 'em to see we belong somewhere else.

PUMPKiN. Oh, Blue – I ain't ready. I ain't no songbird. I can't barely sing in the right key –

BLUE. You got the music in you. I heard it before. You singin' to yourself sometimes.

PUMPKiN. You hear somethin' different than what it really is. I only hummin'. Carry a tune. Maybe sound good till you put me in front of folks.

BLUE. You got to work with Corn. I seen it happen before. Take your potential and turn it into power. Then you and me can make real music together...in Chicago.

PUMPKiN. But I love it here. In Black Bottom. I know folks here and they need me to take care of 'em. I don't wanna leave this and start over somewhere without 'em. Where I ain't got no people. Take a long time for folk to become family.

BLUE. This dead here. Don't you hear me, baby? I need you to take care of me. I'm dyin' here.

PUMPKiN. What about me?

> *(An odd moment. **BLUE** looks at her curiously. **PUMPKiN** quickly realizes her mistake. She tries to fix:)*

I mean, it ain't gonna be no better in Chicago. It's pain everywhere.

BLUE. Not this kinda pain, Pumpkin. *(An admission.)* I can hear her when I play, you know that? I can hear my mama cryin' sometimes and I try to drown her out. But the cryin' get louder and I can't mute it. I can't save her and she remind me over and over.

PUMPKiN. Oh, baby...

BLUE. I hear Daddy too. He comin' to claim me. I ain't gonna be nothin' better and he keep reminding me too. He take my music away and all I got left is chaos.

PUMPKiN. I can love all that chaos away.

BLUE. Will you, baby?

PUMPKiN. I will.

BLUE. Then you'll come with me?

*(**PUMPKIN** retreats.)*

PUMPKIN. What...what about the band?

BLUE. This band? What about it?

PUMPKIN. Everybody here. What they s'pose to do without Paradise? This place our sanctuary.

BLUE. Sanctuary for who??? I'm tellin' you, I ain't right. The damage is in these walls. It's in this club. It's in this band. It's in this whole damn town. I don't want no parts of this no more. Detroit's gonna eat me alive. You hear me? I got to go.

PUMPKIN. Blue. I'll do anything else but I don't wanna leave.

*(Suddenly, **BLUE** grabs hold of **PUMPKIN**'s arms and shakes her.)*

BLUE. Don't say that, Pumpkin. Don't say no / to me –

PUMPKIN. *(Frightened.)* Blue, you hurtin' / me –

BLUE. You got to hear what I'm sayin' / got to understand me –

PUMPKIN. Please, Blue / let me loose.

BLUE. I can't stay here no more – you hear? Don't make me / stay here –

PUMPKIN. Blue / please –

BLUE. Tell me what I want to hear / need to hear –

PUMPKIN. Okay, Blue. / Okay.

BLUE. Tell me you gonna come.

PUMPKIN. I'm gonna come.

BLUE. Say you won't leave me.

PUMPKIN. I won't leave you.

BLUE. I need you, Pumpkin. I need you to keep quiet and don't mention this to none of the fellas till I got the money solid. Don't want them meddlin' and tryin' to mess stuff up. You hear me?

PUMPKIN. Yes, Blue. I hear you.

BLUE. I need you in every way. Touch me like you say and soften the pain. Love it all away so I can be somebody better.

(**BLUE** *releases his grip on* **PUMPKIN** *and drops his head into her lap.*)

(*She kisses his forehead tenderly.*)

PUMPKIN. I will, baby. I will.

(**PUMPKIN** *touches him softly. She massages him on his cheeks, on his hands, on his eyebrows.*)

"For time's deft fingers scroll my brow
With fell relentless art –
I'm folding up my little dreams
Tonight, within my heart."

(**BLUE** *looks up at her and kisses her passionately. Harshly, even. Needfully.*)

(*Lights shift.*)

Scene Five

(Late night. **CORN** *walks into the club carrying something wrapped in foil. He puts his hat on a stand. He heads to the bar, grabs a few napkins and some silverware. Prepares the something wrapped in foil.)*

*(***P-SAM*** *enters the club anxiously.)*

CORN. Where'd you disappear to, Sam? Couldn't find you after the set. But you was right, that String-Finger Charlie was somethin' else.

P-SAM. Told you, didn't I? Ran off to rap with Jimmy the Greek for a minute. Had some news for me.

CORN. What kinda news?

*(***P-SAM*** *looks around for privacy.)*

P-SAM. Corn, I hit it.

CORN. Hit what?

P-SAM. The policy. My number came up. Straight three in a row.

CORN. Well, good for you, Sam. Got you a little bread.

P-SAM. Not no little bread, Corn. A real stash. Something to spread around and get into some serious trouble with.

CORN. You don't wanna be bettin' that on nothin' Sam. Just take your money and make you a little nest somewhere. Don't be like all these other fools done hit the numbers and run out with fur coats and that nonsense.

P-SAM. That ain't what I'm tryin' to do, Corn. I need you to talk to Blue for me.

CORN. Sam, I gotta tell ya – much as I can try to convince Blue on String-Finger Charlie, he ain't gon' be willin' to meet that fee. I can tell you that right now.

P-SAM. That's what I'm sayin' now, Corn. What kinda sense do that make? When you know Blue to be all easy about this band being out of action? Somethin' ain't right about it, and I bet I know what it is.

CORN. Don't go spreadin' stories now, Sam.

P-SAM. He's gonna sell out.

CORN. Blue got roots here. He ain't sellin'.

P-SAM. How much that city talkin' to him for, Corn? They must be offerin' him something nice. Else, Blue got another plan. But it just don't make sense. He ain't even the slightest bit concerned 'bout nothin' but playing solo next Friday. Who you know wanna go on solo that got a quartet? 'Less they fixin' to start playin' with a new one.

CORN. Sam, your mind is runnin' off with your mouth. You makin' stuff up.

P-SAM. I ain't makin' up nothin'. I'm piecing it all together. Jimmy the Greek called it. Said some of these rents over here is gettin' raised. And city payin' off the ones who own. If Blue sellin' out, what's that gonna mean for the rest of us, Corn? No steady bread. No place over our heads. You and me both...unless...

CORN. 'Less what, Sam?

P-SAM. 'Less he sell the club to me instead.

CORN. Blue ain't sellin, Sam.

P-SAM. Just listen here, Corn. I got me enough to make it worth thinkin' about.

CORN. Blue ain't sellin'.

P-SAM. That's all you can say? Blue ain't sellin'. Ain't even gonna listen to nothin' else?

CORN. Blue ain't sellin', and you or nobody else is buyin'. Don't let that Jimmy the Greek get you confused, Sam. Black Bottom ain't lettin' Blue go, even if he want it to.

P-SAM. How you know that, Corn?

CORN. Some stuff I just know.

P-SAM. Just talk to some folks around town, Corn. See if this plan to clean up the city don't mean to clean us out. Get rid of all the niggers. Just like the mayor say in his campaign – *we* the blight he talkin' 'bout. Everybody know Blue's spot is the best spot to take. They get this, they can get everybody else too. One sell out and it weaken the whole bunch. Unless 'steada sellin' to them, we sell to us. I wouldn't be nothin' like Blue. I'd take care of folks over here and give everybody solo time who want it –

CORN. You talkin' takin' over the band too?

P-SAM. I'm tellin' ya, when it's my spot, we all have a pot to piss in. I wouldn't be no cheap, hateful bastard chargin' nickels per ice cube. And I wouldn't let no crackers take from us what we done worked hard to have on our own. I ain't goin' back to playin' background for them big bands. White man say, "Wear this, play this standard, no bop. Smile like this. Sit like this. Take your meal after these folk, nigger." I ain't doin' it, Corn. If this spot was mine, we'd be the kings we supposed to be. I'd tell that new Mayor Cobo to go to hell he wanna take office and clean us out.

CORN. That's enough, Sam. This talk you doin' gonna start a mess of hearsay and send Blue into a mighty rage.

P-SAM. Corn, how long you gon' defend the devil?

CORN. I ain't defending the devil. I'm trying to keep everything smooth. You don't know what I know. You don't know the limits of a man that's on edge like I do. You ain't seen what I seen, Sam. Now I say I'll think on it. That's all I can say to you. But you got to stop this talk now.

P-SAM. You think about it, Corn. And I'll zip my lips. For now.

CORN. Good.

> *(Beat.)*

P-SAM. I'm tempted to go spend a lil' of my winnin's on a fine woman tonight. Maybe try that spiderwoman out for size.

CORN. Not her. You leave her be.

P-SAM. Oh, don't worry 'bout me none. I ain't scared of a lil' poison.

CORN. I say let her 'lone. She ain't got no interest or cause to be talking to you.

(**P-SAM** *looks at* **CORN** *curiously.*)

P-SAM. What's it to you if I bother with her, Corn?

(**CORN** *doesn't respond.* **P-SAM** *smiles knowingly.*)

(*Teasing.*) Oooo! You gon' git bit! She gon' put her pincers in you!

CORN. Cool it out there, Sam.

P-SAM. You wants to get bit – don'tcha? Bet you headed there right now.

CORN. I ain't talkin' on it. She's a sweet woman.

P-SAM. Oh, Corn, don't go gettin' mush over this one. You walkin' a fool line. Them kinda women too much for you.

CORN. I ain't askin' for your permission, Sam. I say she's sweet and I'm done with it.

P-SAM. I bet she sweet. Sweet potato pie. Just keep yo' eyes open, Corn. You can't take no more heartbreak. If she don't know that, the rest of us do. And you think about what I said...about Blue...

CORN. I'll think about it.

P-SAM. Good. I'm gon' stay outta trouble and turn in, myself. Maybe you should too, Corn.

(**P-SAM** *heads off.*)

(*Singing to himself.*)

SWEET POTATO PIIIIEEEEEEE...

(**CORN** *grabs the something wrapped in foil and the silverware.*)

(*Lights shift.*)

Scene Six

(**SILVER** *sits in her room, playing a record on her record player: Charlie "Yardbird" Parker.**)

(She paints her toenails calmly.)

(Suddenly, a knock at her bedroom door.)

(She rises from the vanity and opens it.)

(**CORN** *stands with a bashful smile and extends the something wrapped in foil.)*

CORN. Sweet potato pie was too good to miss.

(**SILVER** *smiles slyly. She takes the pie.)*

SILVER. That's mighty thoughtful of you.

(She cracks open the foil and smells.)

Smell like all kinds of sin. Can't wait to satisfy my sweet tooth.

CORN. I hope you enjoy it well. 'Night, miss.

(**CORN** *turns to leave.)*

SILVER. Wait a minute there, buttercup. Where you goin' so fast?

CORN. I remember you sayin' you wanted to spend the night on your lonesome. I hear a woman say she wanna be left alone, I leave her alone.

SILVER. Well that was before you brought me some sweet potato pie. It ain't no fun to taste sin all alone.

CORN. I really ought not bother you.

SILVER. No bother at all, I say.

(**CORN** *looks at* **SILVER**. *She is the most intriguing beauty he's ever seen. He smiles shyly.)*

---

* A license to produce *Paradise Blue* does not include a performance license for any third-party or copyrighted recordings. Licensees should create their own.

CORN. I suppose...just till you finish your pie...

> (**CORN** *enters the room. He stands.*)

SILVER. Go'on have a seat now.

CORN. Ain't no seat but the bed.

SILVER. My bed bugs don't bite nobody but me. Go'on sit down, sugar.

> (**CORN** *hesitates, but finally takes a seat on the edge of the bed uncomfortably.*)
>
> (**SILVER** *lifts her leg and finishes painting her toes as she talks.* **CORN** *notices the contour of her leg and then tries not to. It's impossible.*)

CORN. This your record player? Brought it with you?

SILVER. Can't go nowhere without my music. A man I'll leave behind. But his music, I'll take forever.

CORN. This here one of my favorites. You play the right stuff.

SILVER. But if you a piano man, you must love some of the Duke, ain't that right?

CORN. Oh, yeah. That's right all right. He's been over to Black Bottom lots of times. Love to hang out in Paradise Valley. Even come by this club a few times.

SILVER. That so?

CORN. It is.

SILVER. What other jazz cats been through here?

CORN. Oh, the best. Mingus. Dizzy. Bird. All the greats. That's somebody I got to play with 'fore I die.

SILVER. Who's that?

CORN. Charlie "Yardbird" Parker. Make me wanna play till my hands fall off.

SILVER. Can't have that. A piano man's hands supposed to be the best hands in the business. Know every curve of a woman cuz the way your hands always stay curved when you play. I imagine you know how to stroke away a lot of ailment, don't you?

CORN. I suppose maybe...

> (**SILVER** *looks at* **CORN** *and smiles. He smiles back. She stands up and spider-walks over to him.*)

SILVER. Lemme see your hands.

> (**SILVER** *takes* **CORN** *by the hands.*)

Yeah...these look like they can play real nice...

> (*She strokes his fingers.*)

CORN. (*Nervously.*) They...they say you been in a lot of cities...

SILVER. (*Calmly.*) Who say that?

CORN. Fff...folks...'round here...

SILVER. I been in a few.

> (**SILVER** *moves closer to* **CORN**. *She strokes his other hand softly.*)

CORN. Ssss...say...you had lots of...mmmm...mmmeen...

SILVER. Awww...not many men. Not too many at all. Just...some...

CORN. Folks 'round here...say...say things...

SILVER. Like what?

CORN. But I don't believe none of it.

SILVER. What they sayin'? I'll tell you whether to believe it or not.

> (**SILVER***'s hand moves to* **CORN***'s leg. He jumps and moves over.*)

CORN. Just say...say you...got secrets...

SILVER. Every woman got secrets.

CORN. Say you like...like a spider...got that Louisana Creole in you...got spirits...

SILVER. You ain't scared of no spiders, is you? Big ol' strong man like you?

CORN. Me?

> (**SILVER** *touches his leg again softly. He is startled...but sits still. Allows it. Enjoys it.*)

Nooooo...no... I lii...liiiike spidersssss...ever since I was a half-pint...collect 'em and watch 'em weave...a...web...

SILVER. You ever been caught in a woman's web?

CORN. Just once.

SILVER. And what happened?

CORN. Fell in love with her. Married her. But she...she died.

> (**SILVER** *stops stroking* **CORN**'s *leg and looks at him compassionately. This is a real moment.*)

SILVER. What was her name?

CORN. Mabel.

SILVER. Was she pretty?

CORN. To me, she was. Most pretty thing I ever saw.

SILVER. How she die?

CORN. Had that TB.

SILVER. Shame.

> (**CORN** *looks at* **SILVER** *sweetly.*)

CORN. You a different kind of woman.

SILVER. Am I?

CORN. Got a bite to you. Sharp. Maybe a little bitter. But you also sweet somewhere too. I can see it in your face. Somewhere you got some sadness.

SILVER. We all got sadness. But I like to turn mine into fire, baby. What you do with yours?

CORN. Play the piano.

SILVER. I'll bet you do.

> (**SILVER** *moves* **CORN**'s *hand to her own thigh.*)

You think you can play this? Find the notes right?

> (**CORN** *keeps his hand stiff.*)

CORN. I...

SILVER. Cuz I need you to find all the blues, and make it sound like bop. Can you do that, buttercup?

CORN. What...what about yo'...pie...

SILVER. I got somethin' taste better 'n that.

> (**SILVER** *straddles* **CORN.** *Puts his hands on her waist.*)

CORN. Whh...what about you? How yo'...husband...die?

> (**SILVER** *moves* **CORN***'s hands to her breast. He gasps...overwhelmed by her allure. She smiles slyly.*)

SILVER. *(Whispering.)* I shot him.

> (*She nibbles his ear.* **CORN** *laughs nervously.*)

Kiss me, daddy.

> (**CORN** *kisses her passionately. They fall back onto the bed.*)

Scene Seven

(Lights up on SILVER's room. It is daytime. The room is empty. A tap-tap comes to her door. No answer. Tap-tap again...)

PUMPKIN. *(From offstage.)* Hello there? Missus Silver? Sheet delivery!

(No answer. The door opens slightly as PUMPKIN peers in.)

Missus Silver?

(Seeing that she isn't in, PUMPKIN enters, carrying a basket of laundry.)

Just gonna make up your bed for you so you have something clean to sleep on. Lord knows what kind of sinful behavior goes on in these sheets, but Pumpkin's gonna starch it all out.

(PUMPKIN starts to remake the bed.)

(She notices some of SILVER's clothing lying around untidily. She folds it and places it in drawers. Hums to herself. The melody has potential, slightly harmonious but meek.)

(PUMPKIN notices more lingerie inside the drawers and pulls out a bit. She looks at SILVER's records.)

(Reading aloud.) Lester Young...

(Looks at the player.)

This is surely a fancy record player. Hope you don't mind if I just...

(She puts a record on the player. "Mean To Me" by Lester Young plays.*)

---

* A license to produce *Paradise Blue* does not include a performance license for "Mean to Me." The publisher and author suggest that the licensee contact ASCAP or BMI to ascertain the music publisher and contact such music publisher to license or acquire permission for performance of the song. If a license or permission is unattainable for

(She peeks back in the drawer and pulls out a bit of lingerie.)

My, my...these things sure are...creative...

(She holds the lingerie up to herself in the mirror. Enjoys it – creates her alter ego.)

(Putting "on.") Hey there, boys. I'm a spiderwoman, and don't none of ya'll come messin' with me 'less you wants to get bit. I'm a gangster woman from Louisiana, and I'll... I'll drink your blood with my chitlins!

(Laughs to herself, snorts a bit.)

I'm a black widow and if you lean too close, I'll stick you right in your Mr. Longleg and suck everything out –

(Gasps with laughter, amazed at her own mouth.)

I'm a... I'm a woman. All you fellas, stop and take a look cuz a real woman done walked in the room. Not nobody to be simple and ignored. Not nobody to be proper and hushed. Not nobody to be uprooted and... *(Pause.)* They call me Silver.

*(**PUMPKIN** studies herself with seriousness. Something in this pretend world starts to feel disturbing.)*

(She regroups and grabs the lingerie. She folds it hastily and tries to organize the drawer.)

(Suddenly she spies something and gasps.)

(She pulls out a gun. It shines in the light.)

*(She freezes. Then she hastily puts the gun back and closes **SILVER**'s drawers.)*

(She grabs her laundry basket.)

---

* "Mean to Me," the licensee may not use the song in *Paradise Blue* but should create an original composition in a similar style or use a similar song in the public domain. For further information, please see Music Use Note on page 3.

(Frazzled, she dashes out of the room.)

(The needle on the record plays on...)

(Lights fade on the room.)

ACT II

Scene One

(Lights up on **BLUE** *playing the trumpet onstage alone. The tune is beautiful but heavy. Loaded with teardrops.)*

*(***SILVER*** enters and watches him.)*

(When he finishes, she applauds. He turns to her sharply.)

SILVER. That's some real fine playin' you doin' / over there.

BLUE. What you doin' down here, woman. Club is closed.

SILVER. Couldn't sleep. So I figure I ought to try goin' for a little walk.

BLUE. This ain't no place for you to wander. Go'on somewhere else.

SILVER. Well now, I figure I'm worth a little preview – don't you think?

BLUE. I say, get the hell outta here.

SILVER. My, my...you sure know how to play rough there, ain't it? Don't trust a woman farther than you can shove her. But I grew up in a house full of bluesmen. Brothers and a daddy. All with bigger ideas of themselves than they was ever able to be. Made 'em angry and frustrated all the time. I ain't lasted this long without knowin' how to play rough right back. *(Shift.)* Say they offerin' ten thousand to folks. You heard that?

BLUE. Didn't I tell you I ain't discussing no business with you?

SILVER. Well, you told me, sho. But men who are contrary always got to say no at the first mention of something. If you smart, you let 'em get that outta the way before you ask for what you really want.

BLUE. And what's that?

SILVER. Your club.

BLUE. It ain't for sell.

SILVER. Everything's for sell. Business. Land. Soul. All it takes is the right price. I can match what this city think they gonna pay you, and add a lil' cherry on top.

BLUE. Match it? You talkin' nonsense. It ain't none of your business what I do, no way.

SILVER. I just wonder what make a person wanna leave somethin' so perfect, seem like. Got Negroes over here runnin' everything and not havin' to answer to nobody but each other. You let this Black Bottom go into the wrong hands, and the soul of this place ain't never gonna forgive you.

BLUE. You shut up now. Talkin' outta line.

(**SILVER** *spider-walks over to* **BLUE** *seductively.*)

SILVER. Can't. Not when I wants something. I got to move on it till I get close enough to stroke it.

(**BLUE** *grabs* **SILVER** *roughly by the arm. She freezes in his grip.*)

BLUE. You wanna take this club out from under me? Hunh? You might got the wool pulled over these fellas' eyes, but I recognize a black widow any way she come. You ain't gonna stick those fangs into me and control me like some prey. You ain't worth the trust I'd give the mayor or the overseer. You out to poison our plans and I ain't gon' let you. This is my Paradise. If I leave, I'm leavin' my way. You got that, woman?

SILVER. I see it in you.

(**BLUE** *looks at her, baffled.*)

Those demons. I see them closing in on you. Choking you, ain't they?

> *(**BLUE** releases **SILVER** and steps back, stunned.)*

My daddy had 'em in him. Husband too. Them feelin's of bein' trapped by yo' skin. Never allowed to get beyond where you at. Turns you mad. Only place you got to escape is that horn, ain't it? But horn only make it louder. Like a dope hit. Got you flyin' and dyin' all in one. I know you, cuz you and me ain't too different. You got contempt like all mens I known. I can dance with contempt and set it aside. But you...it rot to the core. Fill you with demons. Turns you on yo' own kind.

BLUE. Shut up.

SILVER. But you ain't gonna get rid of 'em. They gon' get rid of you. 'Less you make amends.

BLUE. I say shut up!

SILVER. Set this place back in the right motion. Cuz if you don't, them demons gon' eat you alive. And when it done that to my daddy, *(Digging into his soul.)* he lynched himself.

> *(**BLUE** grabs **SILVER** and shakes her.)*

BLUE. I say shut up shut up SHUT UP GOTDAMNIT!

CORN. *(From offstage.)* Blue?

> *(**CORN** enters the club and sees **BLUE**'s hands on **SILVER**. **BLUE** quickly lets **SILVER** go.)*

Blue, what's got you goin'?

> *(**BLUE** is silent. **CORN** stares at **BLUE** and **SILVER**, decoding the event.)*

BLUE. Nothin'. Just down here practicing.

CORN. Pumpkin worried 'bout you. Say you been down here for hours and won't go to bed.

BLUE. Ain't tired.

CORN. Still, Blue. It's late enough. *(Turns to **SILVER**.)* Maybe you should go'on to bed too, sweets. I'll come check on you in a few to make sure you tucked in safe and sound.

(**SILVER** *looks at* **CORN** *and then to* **BLUE**. *She rubs her arm.*)

SILVER. All right, then. (*A moment.*) 'Night, fellas.

(*She heads out of the bar.* **CORN** *looks at* **BLUE** *sternly.*)

CORN. You too, Blue.

BLUE. Can't, Corn. I got to finish. Got to practice more. Ain't there yet.

CORN. Ain't where, Blue?

BLUE. Just ain't there. I'm gon' stay up. I need Friday to be smooth.

CORN. Blue. Pumpkin ain't gettin' no better. Might have to take her off standards. Give her somethin' else to do. I play solo.

BLUE. She got to practice more.

CORN. Practice don't mean nothin' if the music in you too scared to get free. She tryin' her best cuz she know you want her to. But it ain't what she want.

BLUE. Do somethin' else then, Corn. Just make Friday night right. I can't keep on about it. I got to finish workin' here.

(**BLUE** *walks back over to the stage with his trumpet.* **CORN** *watches him.*)

CORN. Blue...you all right, ain't you?

(**BLUE** *ignores this and begins to play a melody.*)

(**CORN** *hesitates for a moment, and then goes to the piano. He joins* **BLUE**'s *melody. A moment of beautiful harmony.*)

(*Quickly, the trumpet goes off-tune. The music stops.* **BLUE** *starts again.* **CORN** *plays again. Another quick beat of harmony. Then the trumpet goes off-tune again. The music stops.*)

It'll come another day, Blue. Not tonight.

BLUE. Hey Corn... What you see when you look at me?

CORN. What you mean, Blue?

BLUE. Don't lie to me.

CORN. I see... A gifted man.

BLUE. Am I fading? Am I...becoming –

CORN. Love Supreme.

BLUE. What?

CORN. That's what you trying to get to, Blue. Love Supreme. That's what he was lookin' for and never found. Your daddy. But you can, Blue. Just not tonight.

> (**BLUE** *takes this in. It's sobering. He turns back to his trumpet. Can't let go the obsession.*)

BLUE. Go on, Corn. Leave me be.

CORN. Don't like seein' you this way, Blue. I... I done seen this happen before –

BLUE. *(Sharply.)* I say leave me!

> *(Silence. **CORN** rises from the piano.)*

> (**BLUE** *remains. He begins to play his tune again. He is transfixed – in his own universe, impervious to* **CORN**. *The trumpet sings an unpleasant melody.* **CORN** *watches for a moment. Then he slowly heads out of the bar.)*

CORN. *(Softly.)* 'Night, Blue...

> *(Lights shift.)*

Scene Two

(Lights up on **PUMPKIN** *and* **P-SAM** *at the bar. She fills his cup of coffee. He eats toast and grits.)*

P-SAM. You put some cinnamon or something in these grits? They taste extra sweet this mornin', Pumpkin.

PUMPKIN. You don't like it?

P-SAM. I ain't sayin' that. Taste a lil' different. But good.

PUMPKIN. I put a dash of cinnamon and a little pinch of brown sugar.

P-SAM. You ain't gonna charge me a extra nickel for that pinch, is you?

PUMPKIN. 'Course I ain't.

P-SAM. Well, then that's all right, Pumpkin. That's all right with me. *(Shift.)* You got some of your pretty words today? I could use somethin' soft like that this mornin'.

PUMPKIN. You mean it? You wanna listen?

P-SAM. 'Course I wanna listen. You think I ain't got no ear like Corn? I can hear the music in them fancy words too. Try me.

PUMPKIN. Okay. Let's see...

*(**PUMPKIN** grabs her book and flips through the pages. She hands it to **P-SAM**.)*

'Kay. Hold the page right there. This one, she calls – "Calling Dreams."
"The right to make my dreams come true
I ask, nay, I demand of life,"

P-SAM. Nay? What's that word?

PUMPKIN. Just um...like "no."

P-SAM. Oh, all right. Go'on Pumpkin.

PUMPKIN. "The right to make my dreams come true
I ask, nay, I demand of life,"

P-SAM. You already said that part, Pumpkin.

PUMPKIN. I was just starting over.

P-SAM. Oh, okay then...you got to say that, Pumpkin. I didn't know that, see?

PUMPKIN. I'm starting over.

P-SAM. Okay. I'm ready for you.

PUMPKIN. "The right to make my dreams come true
I ask, nay, I demand of life,
Nor shall fate's deadly contraband
Impede my steps, nor countermand."

P-SAM. Say it pee on what?

PUMPKIN. Impede.

P-SAM. That ain't what it sound like you was sayin'. It sounded sorta nasty.

PUMPKIN. Impede. I-M-P-E-D-E. To stop something.

P-SAM. Oh, yeah. I see that right here. I got you now. All right – keep goin'.

PUMPKIN. Sam, maybe you ought to just...listen. Maybe not read along.

P-SAM. I can read, Pumpkin.

PUMPKIN. Oh, I know. But maybe the words sound better when you don't read. When you just hear me sayin' 'em to you. That's the magic in it.

P-SAM. All right, then. Gimme the magic.

PUMPKIN. I'm gonna say it all the way through.

P-SAM. I gotcha.

PUMPKIN. No interrupting this time.

P-SAM. *(Zips his lips.)* Locked and sealed.

> *(She takes a breath.)*

I ain't gonna say nothin' else.

> *(She looks at him sternly. He realizes his mistake there. Sits quietly.)*

PUMPKIN. "The right to make my dreams come true
I ask, nay, I demand of life,
Nor shall fate's deadly contraband
Impede my steps, nor countermand.

Too long my heart against the ground
Has beat the dusty years around,
And now, at length, I rise, I wake!
And stride into the morning break!"

(Pause. **P-SAM** *thinks for a second.)*

P-SAM. Pumpkin, I ain't understand a word you just said. But I know one thing, it shoul' do sound like magic when you say it.

PUMPKIN. Thank you, Sam. Just talkin' 'bout...love and dreamin'. That's all you really need to know.

P-SAM. That's somethin' what makes your skin sorta blush. When you say them words.

PUMPKIN. I just like it.

P-SAM. It like you too.

(Beat.)

That's what you should be doin', Pumpkin.

PUMPKIN. What's that?

P-SAM. Puttin' words together. You got a nice way of doin' it. Even if it sound confusing otherwise, you got a way to make it sound like music. I can hear it in you.

PUMPKIN. I ain't no poet. I just like to read it, is all.

P-SAM. How you know, Pumpkin? How you know what you ain't, if you ain't never tried it?

PUMPKIN. I don't know, I... You think I make it sound like music?

P-SAM. Like a songbird. You could be like them Harlem cats. Puttin' them words on paper and in books. Be real classy and smart. That's what you are. Ain't Blue never told you that?

PUMPKIN. I'm fine just working here. Taking care of folks. I like taking care of folks. It's what I'm good at.

P-SAM. Woman like you shouldn't have to take care of nobody. Man should be takin' care of you.

PUMPKIN. I'm okay just being here with Blue.

P-SAM. But is Blue okay just being here with you?

(Beat. **PUMPKIN** *is affected. She shifts and starts clearing* **P-SAM***'s plate.)*

PUMPKIN. Gonna take this for you now, if you're done. Get to cleanin' the dishes and finishin' the laundry.

P-SAM. Why when I get to talkin' 'bout Blue, you get to talkin' 'bout dirty laundry? Why you can't just answer me straight?

PUMPKIN. I got a lot of stuff to do.

P-SAM. I see you every day lookin' just as pretty and simple as you can be, and I think of all the things I'd like to give you. All the ways you could fit right in with what I wanna do. You a go-along gal.

PUMPKIN. A go-along gal.

P-SAM. And I like that. Don't make much fuss about nothin'. Just wanna make life easy for a man. And I can do somethin' with that.

PUMPKIN. I got a life with Blue.

P-SAM. What kinda life, Pumpkin? Cleanin' his dirty drawers? You ain't got no real life with Blue. But you could have one with me.

PUMPKIN. Sam, you shouldn't talk like that.

*(***P-SAM*** moves closer to* **PUMPKIN***.)*

P-SAM. I'm just talkin' the truth, Pumpkin.

PUMPKIN. But I don't love you.

P-SAM. You'll learn to.

PUMPKIN. I don't want to.

P-SAM. You need to.

PUMPKIN. It ain't right.

*(***P-SAM*** is close enough to* **PUMPKIN** *to feel her breath.)*

P-SAM. It ain't wrong neither. It's somewhere in between.

PUMPKIN. Sam, I can't.

P-SAM. Hear that, Pumpkin? You called me – Sam.

*(***P-SAM*** tries to kiss* **PUMPKIN***. She smacks his face.)*

PUMPKIN. Damnit I say no!

> (**SILVER** *enters the bar slowly.*)

> (**P-SAM** *takes the hint. Backs off.*)

SILVER. Mornin', folks.

PUMPKIN. *(Startled.)* Oh – mornin', Missus. Was just bringing up your breakfast in a sec.

SILVER. No, nevermind. I'll just have some juice right down here. That's all I need this mornin'.

PUMPKIN. Gettin' it for you right now. Bring you out another coffee too, Sam.

> (**SILVER** *walks over to* **P-SAM** *and sits beside him. He slumps in his stool.*)

SILVER. Doll, you look like you could use a lil' sugar in your coffee this mornin'. Need somethin' sweet.

P-SAM. I done had enough sweet for today. *(Pause.)* I'll take somethin' spicy instead.

SILVER. That right?

P-SAM. Yeah, that's right, all right. *(Shift.)* Say, I hear you been askin' 'round 'bout business over here. You got ambitions for Black Bottom?

SILVER. Heard that, did you?

P-SAM. I did. Notice you been talkin' with my buddy a bit. Spendin' a lot of time.

SILVER. See through walls, can you?

P-SAM. I see smiles on a face ain't smiled like that in years. Only one kind of thing be responsible for that.

SILVER. What of it.

P-SAM. Maybe you can put him up to somethin' for me. Somethin' what'll benefit us all. I done put the bug in his ear to talk to Blue for me, but I gots a feelin' you more persuasive than me. And maybe there's a shot you an' me can do some business together. If you can fancy that.

SILVER. You know, sugar…from what I seen – too many names on a dotted line cause too much confusion. The plans I got is for my signature only.

(**P-SAM** *is taken aback.*)

P-SAM. Oh, you too good to be partners. I get it. Well, Blue ain't sellin' this club to neither one of us without some muscle behind 'im. And I tell you this, if you ain't on this with me, then you competition. We got an order to the line sweetheart, be careful 'bout tryin' to take cuts. *(Shift.)* Tell Pumpkin I said no need for the coffee. Ain't nothin' in here for me today.

(**P-SAM** *walks off.*)

(**PUMPKIN** *comes in from the kitchen with juice and coffee. She notices* **P-SAM** *is gone.*)

PUMPKIN. Where's Sam?

SILVER. Say he had to go.

(**PUMPKIN** *hands* **SILVER** *her juice and looks at her uneasily.* **SILVER** *watches* **PUMPKIN** *quietly.*)

Thought you might have time to teach me a bit of that fancy poetry of yours.

PUMPKIN. *(Sharply.)* Can't. Busy. Got laundry.

SILVER. Oh. Well... *(Pause.)* Maybe later then.

PUMPKIN. Can't. Busy then too.

SILVER. I see.

(**SILVER** *is onto* **PUMPKIN** *as* **PUMPKIN** *does a bad job of busying herself. She tries to corner* **PUMPKIN**.)

That's too bad. Maybe next time.

PUMPKIN. Um. We'll have to see...

(**PUMPKIN** *scurries out, narrowly missing* **SILVER**'s *web.* **SILVER** *calls after her.*)

SILVER. Hope your wrists are feeling better!

(**SILVER** *sits, disturbed that* **PUMPKIN** *got away. She puts money on the bar and exits, unsettled...*)

Scene Three

(Dim lights up on **BLUE** *and* **PUMPKIN** *in the bar.* **BLUE** *plays his trumpet and* **PUMPKIN** *sits, drinking tea as she listens.)*

(Lights up on **SILVER** *and* **CORN** *in* **SILVER**'s *bed. They are in the afterglow of lovemaking.)*

*(***BLUE** *plays softly in the bar. The two worlds exist simultaneously.)*

*(***SILVER** *smokes a cigarette.* **CORN** *caresses her.)*

CORN. You got the prettiest skin. Like honey – smooth. Taste like it too.

*(***CORN** *kisses* **SILVER**'s *arm. She smiles at him.)*

And your arms. Can feel the shape of all your womanness in your arms.

*(***SILVER** *blows a puff of smoke.)*

SILVER. Has it been that long, sugar?

CORN. Since what?

SILVER. Since you felt the touch of a woman?

CORN. Not since Mabel died.

SILVER. That's goin' on three years now. Ain't it? How you stay away from women so long?

CORN. Thought that part was dead. Till you come along and wake it up.

SILVER. I got a way of wakin' up a lot of things in men. It ain't always good. *(Shift.)* Did you do what I asked you?

CORN. I ain't talk to him just yet. He on edge 'bout this gig. After the show be better.

SILVER. Friday may be too late. He mighta already signed those papers by then.

CORN. I got to give him his chance to find what he lookin' for. Then I'll know what to do. Don't worry 'bout him sellin'.

SILVER. I know when a man is close to breakin', and I see that in your buddy.

CORN. What you askin' ain't easy.

SILVER. But it's necessary.

CORN. There's more to it than just sellin'. I knowed Blue a long time. Knew his daddy, name was Clyde Sr. What Blue don't tell nobody is he Clyde Jr. But better not call him that. He liable to pull his knife on you. Clyde Sr. gave me a shot. Let me play with the house band to keep from runnin' the streets. He made a legacy of Paradise Club, and Blue been trying to hold it together, but lately...

SILVER. Daddy got a cloud over him, don't he?

*(In the bar, **BLUE**'s tune changes. A melody of difficulty. It grows increasingly heavy.)*

CORN. Blue's daddy had that thing where his mind wasn't always right. Sometimes be talkin' to himself or to somebody who wun'nt there. But the man could play a trumpet like he was touched by God. And Blue got that same gift in him. But it come with a whole lot of extra. And that extra ate his daddy alive till he killed Blue's mama when Blue was a young man. Said he saw the devil trying to take her, and he was tryin' to save her.

SILVER. My / God...

CORN. So he strangled her to death. Blue seen the whole thing. And his daddy wind up in the crazy house. That where he died. Blue been carryin' all that with him ever since.

SILVER. That kinda dead weight make a man dangerous. It can turn on you.

CORN. Blue ain't a bad man. He just wanna be mighty but the world keep him small. Cost of bein' colored and gifted. Brilliant and second class. Make you insane.

SILVER. He's divin' deeper than most. Don't you see that much?

CORN. Been seein' it for a while. He gettin' worser. But I know what he needs.

SILVER. What's that.

CORN. Love Supreme. That's what we call it when you hit that perfect note that cleans your sins. Like white light bathin' him with mercy. It's that part in the music that speak directly to God, and you ready to play with the angels.

SILVER. When you got demons that deep, they don't redeem you. They kill you to the soul. Believe me, I know. It's time for him to move on 'fore that happen.

CORN. What you want to run a club for, hunh? You stay here with me, and I'll make sure you don't need nothin' else.

SILVER. You talk like this gonna be somethin' permanent.

CORN. Isn't it?

(**SILVER** *looks at* **CORN** *questioningly.*)

SILVER. Doll, listen here, I done learned from enough men not to settle my bags in anybody's heart too long. Cuz it start off good, but sooner or later I ain't gonna be able to fill all your needs. And then it's gonna be heartbreak city. I spare myself and you the pain.

CORN What make you think I need anything else but this?

SILVER. Men always do. And I can't give it, baby.

CORN. Why can't you?

SILVER. Cuz I'm broke. And ain't no fixin' me.

CORN. I like broke.

SILVER. Not like this.

CORN. How you know?

SILVER. Cuz I'm cursed.

CORN. What you mean?

SILVER. Childless. Can't have 'em. Body just cursed.

(**BLUE**'*s melody changes to a more aggressive rhythm.*)

(**CORN** *looks at* **SILVER**. *He touches her stomach. She moves his hand.*)

Ain't nothin' but dead in there, baby. Don't no life happen here. Couldn't give none to my husband and he hated me for it. Cursed me to hell, he did. And almost sent me straight there, too. But I got out of that. I'm here and I'm fightin' for my piece at life. What's a woman if she ain't bearing fruit? Ain't no other place for her in this world 'less she runnin' her own business. Got to find another way to be fruitful. I ain't gonna be nothin' frail to get preyed on. I'm gon' do the preying if it's any to be done. And this Paradise Club is ripe for the taking. So come on, baby. Tell me you gonna talk to him, so I can be something more than just childless.

CORN. And then what happens to this? Us here?

SILVER. You gon' be the headliner, baby. I'll see to that.

CORN. I wanna be the headliner right here.

> (**CORN** *touches her heart.*)

Break the curse. I can do that for you, if you let me.

> (**SILVER** *touches* **CORN**'s *hand, then his face.*)

SILVER. You must really like the taste of pain, don't you?

> (*He answers her with a kiss.*)

> (**BLUE**'s *horn leaps in volume.*)

> (**SILVER** *and* **CORN** *fall back onto the bed as lights crossfade to* **PUMPKIN** *and* **BLUE**.)

> (**BLUE**'s *final note moves from passionate to broken. He pushes again. It becomes piercing.*)

> (**PUMPKIN** *drops her teacup. It shatters.*)

> (**BLUE**'s *note pierces. Pierces. Pierces.*)

> (**PUMPKIN** *rushes over to him as he blows his trumpet. She tries to stop him but he keeps on. The note pierces.*)

PUMPKIN. (*Screaming.*) Blue!

(She extends her arm and he pushes it away.)

(Screaming over the notes.) Blue, baby! Please!

> *(**BLUE** pierces more, almost in a trance. A battle between him and his trumpet. Fighting something in the notes.)*

> *(**PUMPKIN** tries to grab hold of him, tugs at his arm. His trumpet falls.)*

BLUE. Nooooooooooooooooo!!!!!!!!!!!!!!!!!!!!!!!!!!!!!!!!!

> *(He shakes her and pushes her violently. She flies into the tables and onto the ground.)*

Let her go – motherfucker! Let her go!

> *(He picks up a chair and throws it recklessly.)*

> *(Then he falls to the ground and wails.)*

> *(**PUMPKIN** lies still. Alive and alert but frightened.)*

(Muttering.) I couldn't-could-couldn't stop stop stop it...couldn't-save-save-her-couldn't-fight-back-fight-back-fight him him him – couldn't-didn't-do-nothing nothing nothing.

PUMPKIN. *(Softly.)* Blue...

BLUE. Killed...killed-her-killed-her her her I – did – I – did – was me me me.

PUMPKIN. Wasn't you...

BLUE. Was me me me... I'm gone...gone...gone...

PUMPKIN. Blue, it's all right...

BLUE. I'm gone...gone...dead...dead...dead...

PUMPKIN. You alive, Blue, baby. You here with me. With Pumpkin.

BLUE. Pumpkin?

> *(**BLUE** stops. He looks at **PUMPKIN**...like a stranger. As if it's his first time seeing her.)*

Pumpkin, I'm dead. I'm not here. They got me, Pumpkin. Stole my soul. I scream to 'em and they scream back. Won't let me forget. Won't silence. I can't hear the notes in the scale. I'm outside myself watchin', but I can't get in. It took me, Pumpkin. The madness took me.

> (**PUMPKIN** *slowly goes over to* **BLUE**. *She kneels beside him.*)

You're gonna leave me, Pumpkin.

PUMPKIN. What, Blue? Why would you think –

BLUE. You love this place more than you love me and I ain't gonna be able to stop you. I ain't gonna have nothin' left. I'm gonna die here, Pumpkin. If I don't get out soon, I'm gonna die.

PUMPKIN. If we leave here, Blue, you really think the hurtin'a stop? I mean, ALL of it?

BLUE. It got to, Pumpkin.

PUMPKIN. Even...with me?

BLUE. It just got to.

> (**PUMPKIN** *considers.*)

PUMPKIN. Okay, Blue. I ain't gonna let Black Bottom hurt you no more.

> (**BLUE** *grabs* **PUMPKIN** *and falls in her lap.*)

> (**PUMPKIN** *holds him strangely, unsettled...*)

Scene Four

> (**SILVER**'s *room. Evening light spills through the windows.* **SILVER** *listens to* Bird and Diz* *on the record player. A soft tap at the door.*)

PUMPKIN. *(From offstage.)* Missus, I got your supper with me. Just gonna leave it for you out here.

> (**SILVER** *goes to the door and opens it.*)

SILVER. Come on in here, honey. Let me talk to you for a sec.

PUMPKIN. I got a lot of other deliveries to make. And the kitchen is a mess –

SILVER. Only for a sec? Could use a lil' girl talk –

PUMPKIN. I still gotta go straighten the bar, and then meet with Corn so I can get ready –

SILVER. I know you been through my things.

> (**PUMPKIN** *freezes for a second, and then quickly enters the room – closing the door behind her.*)

PUMPKIN. It was only an accident –

SILVER. 'Course it was.

PUMPKIN. I didn't mean to be inconsiderate. I just came to change the sheets –

SILVER. And listen to a little Lester Young and sort through my drawers.

PUMPKIN. I didn't –

SILVER. Relax, honey. No need to worry so. I ain't mad at you.

PUMPKIN. It was a terrible mistake and I swear I won't do it again.

SILVER. You see somethin' you like? Want it for ya'self?

---

* A license to produce *Paradise Blue* does not include a performance license for any third-party or copyrighted music. Licensees should create an original composition or use music in the public domain. For further information, please see Music Use Note on page 3.

PUMPKIN. Oh, no, Missus. No, I don't want to bother in any more of your things.

SILVER. You sho?

PUMPKIN. Yes, ma'am.

SILVER. Cuz I figure you musta got a lil' curious 'bout somethin'. And I can take all that curiosity away right now.

PUMPKIN. No, I'm fine. Really.

SILVER. Just let you have a lil' look-see.

> (**SILVER** *pulls out the gun. It shines in the light.* **PUMPKIN** *gasps.*)

This what you so 'fraid of? This lil' bitty thing?

PUMPKIN. *(Nervously.)* I... I don't need to see that, Missus. It's your...private –

SILVER. Ain't too private no more. Or is it? You tell me.

PUMPKIN. I ain't...told nobody...

SILVER. No? Not even yo' man?

PUMPKIN. No...nobody...

SILVER. Hunh... *(Pause.)* Well, that's good, then. Men find out a woman got a gun, they ready to lock her in a dungeon and throw away the key.

PUMPKIN. Why you...why you have it?

SILVER. For protection.

PUMPKIN. Protection from who?

SILVER. Anybody. Everybody. You think a woman can move on her lonesome from town to town without the know-how to put a bullet in somebody's head?

PUMPKIN. That ain't for a lady to do.

SILVER. Says who?

PUMPKIN. That's why a woman ain't supposed to be on her lonesome. Travel with a man by your side and he be all the protection you need.

SILVER. That so? That what your man do for you? Make you feel protected and safe?

PUMPKIN. 'Course he does.

SILVER. That why you got those bruises on your arm?

> (**PUMPKIN** *falls silent.*)

Seem to me like you ain't no safer than me on my lonesome. In fact, I'll say I'm the better of us two. Cuz I know how to shoot straight and aim direct. And I ain't shy when I got this in my hand, neither. Ain't no wallflower. I'm front and center on the floor. And I ain't afraid to use it. That's where people get you. They see you got it but don't 'spect you to use it. But once somebody see yo' gun, they done seen all your cards right there on the table. So you either fold, or you take the win. And me, I always take the win.

PUMPKIN. What happened to yo' husband?

SILVER. That's a tale for another day.

PUMPKIN. Why you move here on your lonesome?

SILVER. I told you, he died.

PUMPKIN. How he die?

SILVER. Bullet in the head.

> (**SILVER** *looks at* **PUMPKIN** *– who has now scrunched herself up in a corner.*)

Now gal, why you so far over there? What you so 'fraid of? Ain't you never held one of these before?

> (**PUMPKIN** *is still.*)

Well, goodness, come on. Let me be your first.

> (**PUMPKIN** *is still.* **SILVER** *laughs.*)

You think I'm gon' shoot you? *(Laughing.)* Don't you think I woulda done that by now?

PUMPKIN. I really...should be...going now...

SILVER. All right now, that's enough.

> (**SILVER** *walks over to* **PUMPKIN** *and grabs her hand.*)

You can't be a prissy lil' thing all yo' life. Sometimes you got to learn some other tricks. Grab it.

PUMPKIN. No, Missus, I can't –

SILVER. I say, grab it!

> (**PUMPKIN** *takes the gun timidly. She holds it like it smells.*)

It ain't dirty drawers. You got to hold it. Give it a grip.

PUMPKIN. I don't want to.

SILVER. Here. Like this.

> (**SILVER** *moves behind* **PUMPKIN** *and puts her hands over* **PUMPKIN***'s hands.*)

You got to hold it firm. It's a delicate egg. Too tight make it bust. Not tight enough and it slip right out your hands. Got it?

> (**PUMPKIN** *nods. She holds the gun.*)

Now you don't wanna put your finger by that trigger too soon. Hold it up here.

> (**SILVER** *moves* **PUMPKIN***'s finger.*)

You do it too early, and you liable to blow somebody's brains out just for sayin' good morning.

PUMPKIN. My arm feels heavy.

SILVER. You ain't used to it, that's all. When you get used to carrying it, won't feel like nothin' but another piece of you. Your best friend.

PUMPKIN. This ain't got nothin' in it, has it?

SILVER. You think I'm fool enough to give you a loaded gun?

PUMPKIN. My arm's gettin' tired.

SILVER. Hold it straight. Support it with your other hand. On the bottom. Like this.

> (**SILVER** *places* **PUMPKIN***'s hands properly.*)

PUMPKIN. I'm breathin' funny.

SILVER. That ain't nothin' but power and nerves runnin' through your blood. Mixin' all together. Feel almost thrillin'. Like holdin' a man's Mr. Happy in your hand.

PUMPKIN. You speak so dirty!

SILVER. Feels good. Try it.

PUMPKIN. I can't.

SILVER. Just say somethin'.

PUMPKIN. Like what?

SILVER. Anything that comes out. You can say what you want with a gun in your hand.

PUMPKIN. I don't know what to say.

SILVER. Tell somebody to move out your way.

PUMPKIN. Move outta my way.

SILVER. Even with that gun you ain't scarin' nobody. Say it like you mean it.

PUMPKIN. Move outta my way!

SILVER. Good. Now tell 'em they better not mess with you or you'll shoot their balls right off 'em.

PUMPKIN. I can't say that.

SILVER. Say it now! Go'on!

PUMPKIN. Don't you mess me with me or I'll shoot you right in your –

SILVER. Balls.

PUMPKIN. So nasty.

SILVER. Say it.

PUMPKIN. I can't!

SILVER. Balls! Go'on. I'll shoot you in your –

PUMPKIN. It's too nasty –

SILVER. Scream it! I'll shoot you in your –

PUMPKIN. Balls! Balls balls balls! In your balls!

> (**SILVER** *bursts out laughing.* **PUMPKIN** *laughs too. They crack up for a moment.*)

SILVER. My goodness! You got a dirty mouth.

PUMPKIN. I sound silly.

> (**PUMPKIN** *sets the gun down.*)

SILVER. Sound silly at first. But the more you believe it, the more everybody else will too. Take time, but you soon learn.

PUMPKIN. I don't need to learn. I'm not gonna be like you. Not movin' from town to town lettin' anybody in my bed who fits the season. Can't make no home that way.

SILVER. You can't make a home your way neither.

(**SILVER** *grabs* **PUMPKIN***'s wrist and* **PUMPKIN** *flinches.*)

How many times he put his hands on you today?

PUMPKIN. I need to get goin' –

SILVER. Is it every day? Or just whenever he got troubles?

PUMPKIN. That's none of your / concern, Missus.

SILVER. Don't matter whether or not it's my concern. I know what I see. And I tell you one thing, gal. You in a heap of trouble if you think you 'bout to make a life with this man. A man with demons ain't gonna see you as nothin' but a gateway to hell. Whenever them spirits come callin', he got to fight anybody they tell him to. And if you in his way, then he gonna fight you.

PUMPKIN. Blue got troubles, yes. But every man got troubles. We take it and we ease it much as possible. That's what a woman do. 'Sides, Black Bottom is the source of most of it. Soon a change gon' come and make things better for 'im.

SILVER. Waitin' on a man to change is like waitin' for the seventh sign. When it comes, it's gonna bring a whole lotta destruction with it. I wouldn't wait for that if I was you.

PUMPKIN. He's a good man. I know you don't see that, but he is. Use' to court me at the main library on Woodward. Love goin' there to study when I was schoolin'. The architecture...those majestic steps. Blue come to walk me home every day after I finish my reading. Wait for me on those steps like I was royalty. He be there with his trumpet in his hand and play for me when I walk out the door. That's when I first seen it. This man has a gift. The kind that make you feel like somebody just to be close to it. Sometimes his lovin' hurts, true. But when it feels good, it feel like heaven. Even if just half as good, that's better than nothin'.

SILVER. A gift is good. But a gift can blind you. Don't get no man's gift confused with that man in the flesh.

PUMPKIN. You don't know him.

SILVER. I know men.

PUMPKIN. Blue ain't all men.

SILVER. He's a man. Men is men.

PUMPKIN. Things'll change soon.

SILVER. You'll be dead 'fore they do.

PUMPKIN. I can't move like you. It ain't me. I like soft words and taking care of folks. You got your way to make it through and I got mine. I know how to make a man feel safe and that's my trade. I'm a go-along gal.

SILVER. That ain't you. That's just the make-up you wear. You a thinkin' woman with her own words. But you play these mens just the same as me. Make 'em feel safe so they make you feel safe. But doll, ain't none of us really safe. No matter what they tell you.

PUMPKIN. Blue just ailing right now. Ain't we all?

SILVER. You want to keep ailin' with him??? Or you want it to stop? Tell me now. True.

PUMPKIN. I...

I want it to stop.

SILVER. Then make it.

PUMPKIN. How?

(**SILVER** *moves calmly.*)

SILVER. Get you a revolver.

PUMPKIN. What?

SILVER. Or you can borrow mine.

PUMPKIN. What d'you mean?

SILVER. Woman got to put her foot down sometimes. Or it ain't never gonna stop. Sometimes, only thing can make it stop is a bullet.

*(**PUMPKIN** looks at **SILVER** – stunned.)*

PUMPKIN. You're...not serious...

SILVER. I'm bein' straight.

PUMPKIN. I would never...

SILVER. Keep it in your stocking. Under your pillow. In your boudoir. Wherever you can get to it.

PUMPKIN. I would never do that.

SILVER. Or carry it in your purse –

PUMPKIN. I say I would NEVER!!!

SILVER. You don't know what you would do till it's just you, him and the devil. Trust me, gal. You don't know.

PUMPKIN. Where would I even...

...

...

No. No, I don't want to think about this. You a filthy dirty Creole woman and everything they say about you is true. You just tryin' to poison me.

> *(**PUMPKIN** walks to the door and opens it. She stops and turns back to **SILVER**.)*

Yo' husband... How he die?

> *(**SILVER** pulls a cigarette from her bosom and lights it.)*

You a sick woman.

SILVER. Any man put his hands on a woman is asking to be shot. Straight between the eyes. And if you know what's good for you, you betta get your gun.

> *(**PUMPKIN**, caught between astonishment and intrigue, storms out of the room.)*

> *(**SILVER** takes a long...long...long...drag...)*

Scene Five

(A horn plays in the distance. It is **BLUE**. *He stands in silhouette, as he did in the beginning of the play. He struggles through his horn and slowly starts to find the notes. It is not perfect, but there is something on track about it. Something promising.)*

(Lights come up on Paradise Club. The floor and bartop glisten. The place looks pristine and ready for opening.)

*(***CORN*** sits at the piano playing a soft tune.)*

*(***PUMPKIN***, dressed simply, recites a poem. It is almost musical. She begins meekly, but then – as if the truth of the words overwhelms her – she gains increasing vocal power. She is half reciting, half singing. She sounds amazing.)*

(As **CORN** *plays underneath her, they become perfectly harmonious.)*

PUMPKIN.
I WANT TO REACH YOU SOFTLY
TOUCH YOU WHERE YOU AIL
LIFT YOU IN YOUR SADNESS
WINDS BENEATH YOUR SAIL

I WANT TO REACH YOU PURELY
IN TRUTH AND LOVE SUBLIME
I BECOME THE SUN
COME CASCADE IN MY SHINE

I WANT TO REACH YOU DEEPLY
MY PALM UPON YOUR CORE
RELEASING EVERY DARKNESS
UNTIL YOU ACHE NO MORE...*

---

* A license to produce *Paradise Blue* does not include music. The author intends that licensees should create their own composition.

(**CORN** *stops. He beams at her.*)

CORN. That was good, Pumpkin.

PUMPKIN. Think so?

CORN. That's the music in you. You found it. That those Miss Johnson woman's words open you like that?

PUMPKIN. Not this time, Corn. (*A small admission.*) My own.

CORN. You wrote that one yourself, Pumpkin?!

PUMPKIN. Think it'll be okay for this evenin' 'stead of the standards?

CORN. I believe it's worth the try.

(**SILVER** *enters the bar.* **PUMPKIN** *spots her.*)

PUMPKIN. Well, then… I better go get dressed 'fore we open.

(**PUMPKIN** *walks passed* **SILVER** *briskly.* **SILVER** *eyes her carefully, then turns to* **CORN.**)

SILVER. Your playin' sound real good, sweets. You 'bout ready for this evenin'?

CORN. About. Got to finish suitin' up, but I feel like Pumpkin gonna be all right –

SILVER. That's not what I mean. You know what I'm talking about.

(*Pause.*)

CORN. Like I told you: tonight. After. Not before. Too much going on before.

SILVER. We better hope after ain't too late.

CORN. You think about what I said too? 'Bout you and me?

SILVER. I did.

CORN. So is that a yes?

SILVER. Well… (*Sincerely.*) it ain't a no.

(**P-SAM** *enters the club loudly, a hint of intoxication in his walk. He approaches the bar.*)

P-SAM. Well…look at this place. Look like a real happenin' spot tonight, don't it?

CORN. Hey there, Sam. You all right?

P-SAM. Is I'm all right? Ain't that the question-of-the-motherfuckin'-year. Is I'm all right? Let's see there, Corn. I ain't got no gig. I ain't got no woman. And I'm drunk on some three-penny wine from Alfie's Liquor Sto'. What you think, Corn? That sound all right?

CORN. Sam, you ain't lookin' good.

P-SAM. Well, nigger, you ain't lookin' good neither. You lookin' like a backstabbing fink if I ever saw one.

SILVER. Maybe I should freshen up for the show.

P-SAM. Freshen up good, baby. Cuz Sammy know all about yo' tricks. Go'on put on some of that rose-smellin' perfume and them sugar-tastin' drawers that got my buddy here all dumbstruck.

> (**CORN** *squares off with* **P-SAM.**)

CORN. Sam, watch your mouth there.

> (**SILVER** *holds out her hand to stop* **CORN.**)

SILVER. It's okay, sweets. We'll finish this later.

> (*She exits.* **P-SAM** *looks after her with contempt, then turns back to* **CORN.**)

P-SAM. Was she worth it, Corn? Was the cootie worth it?

CORN. What you talkin' 'bout, Sam?

P-SAM. Nigger, don't be tryin' to play dumb on me. I ain't no clown.

CORN. I never say you was a clown –

P-SAM. You sold me up the river! You think I don't know?

CORN. Sam –

P-SAM. You double-crossed me, damnit!

CORN. Wait a minute, Sam. What you mean?

P-SAM. You know what I mean. That spiderwoman got your nostrils stretched so tall they blockin' yo' eyesight! You cuttin' side deals on me with her, ain't that it?

CORN. I just told her like I told you. I'm gon' talk to Blue and see if he'll listen to what you have to say. Both of you.

P-SAM. Both of us, hunh? And that's it? No leanin' him no particular way?

CORN. That's it, Sam.

P-SAM. Corn, you a lyin' monkey. I ain't never thought I'd see the day when you look me straight in the eye and lie. I guess that's what happen when you get bit by the bug, ain't it. But you done messed up now. You so busy cuttin' side deals you ain't keep yo' eyes on the prize. And that nigger sold it! Just like I say!

CORN. Sold what, Sam? Paradise??? Nawww...that can't be. Blue ain't leavin' this spot –

P-SAM. That's bullshit, Corn! He done already left it! Ask these other clubs – they all seen it. Blue's name on the list of sellers. Gave his word and the handshake and signin' this club over on Monday. Monday! That's three days from now. And along with him goes Percy at Garfield's Lounge, and Harold from Three Sixes. Even the Norwood Hotel gettin' bought out with this new plan. It's just like I was tellin' you. You get one – you get 'em all. And Blue done started a train wreck we coulda stopped if you'da been keepin' your ear to the ground 'steada up in some crazy woman's cooter.

CORN. Hold on, Sam. Monday ain't here yet. That mean he ain't signed it. A list ain't nothin' but a promise. We don't know the real plan 'less we hear it from Blue hisself.

P-SAM. Listen at you – hear it from Blue. You gon' trust Blue over half of Black Bottom?

CORN. If what they say is true, I got to hear it from Blue's mouth. See it in his eyes. Then I'll know what I know.

P-SAM. Then let's get it from his mouth then! Call him right now. Blue! Blue!!! Bring your sellout tail down here, nigger!

CORN. Sam!

(**PUMPKIN** *enters. She is dressed in a stunning red gown with red painted lips and a rose in her hair. She is breathtaking.*)

PUMPKIN. Sam? What's the matter down here?

P-SAM. Pumpkin, this ain't none of your –

(**P-SAM** *sees* **PUMPKIN** *for the first time – fully. He is caught off guard.*)

– concern...

CORN. It's all right, Pumpkin. Sam just a little drunk.

P-SAM. *(To* **PUMPKIN**.*)* You look...good...

PUMPKIN. Thank you, Sam.

CORN. Pumpkin, where's Blue?

PUMPKIN. Gettin' his suit on. Upstairs. Should be down in a sec.

CORN. I'm gonna go get him and we'll settle this once and for all.

(**CORN** *heads off.* **P-SAM** *stares at* **PUMPKIN**, *mesmerized.*)

P-SAM. Pumpkin, I ain't never seen you so...done up.

PUMPKIN. Tonight is special, Blue say. Had to look classy.

P-SAM. You look too classy for Blue. Hell, too classy for every fella in Black Bottom. You deserve the top-of-the-line. Somewhere you can write your poems and won't have to clean one dirty dish. Get you a maid to do that.

PUMPKIN. I don't need none of that, Sam. I'm fine right here.

P-SAM. Why you fine like this, Pumpkin? Just tell me and I'll let you be. Why you won't even let me pretend to give you nothin' better?

PUMPKIN. I don't know, Sam. I don't know why I can't love you. I think you so sweet sometimes. I like to laugh with you. And I do wonder what it'll be like if I closed my eyes and just let you in. I listen to the way you drum and it sound so scattered and rough. Somehow, it works for that bop sound. But for my ear, it just don't sound like a trumpet. When I hear that horn, I get lost in its pain and its beauty. It speak to me different. I just don't know how to change what my ear is favorable to.

P-SAM. I sho wish I did, Pumpkin. I wish I knew how to turn you to my kinda sound.

(**PUMPKIN** *looks at* **P-SAM** *sincerely.*)

PUMPKIN. You a good man, Sam.

P-SAM. It sound so right when you call me that.

(**PUMPKIN** *touches* **P-SAM**'s *face gently. He softens to her touch. She smiles.*)

(**BLUE** *walks in, with* **CORN** *at his heels.*)

(**BLUE** *storms over to* **PUMPKIN** *and grabs her roughly by the arm.*)

BLUE. What kinda game you playin' at? You tryin' to make a fool outta me?

PUMPKIN. No, no... Blue, I –

P-SAM. Let her be!

(**P-SAM** *grabs* **BLUE**'s *arm and turns him around.* **BLUE** *snatches his arm back.*)

BLUE. What the hell you want here, nigger.

P-SAM. I wanna hear you tell it, that's what. Tell Corn and everybody up in here how you sold us out.

BLUE. I ain't got to tell nobody nothin'.

P-SAM. You gon' say it, goddamnit. You gonna tell everybody how you put Paradise Club on the list to be sold for ten thousand dollars. Gonna sign it over on Monday. You tell Corn right now, nigger!

BLUE. I ain't tellin' you jack.

CORN. Blue, tell him you ain't sellin'.

BLUE. I ain't got to tell him a motherfuckin' thing, Corn. Nigger come up in here like I owe him somethin'. I don't owe nobody nothin', you hear me? I do what I wanna do cuz it's my place! Ain't nobody got to live with my madness but me, you hear me?

P-SAM. You? You you you you YOU! Everything always about YOU! But this ain't just *your* club. You might be the one to own it, but you ain't the one to make it. We all make this Paradise. You wouldn't have nothin' to stand on all this time if it wun'nt for me, Corn and Joe backing you up and makin' you sound good.

BLUE. Makin' me sound good?

P-SAM. You wouldn't have no club if it wun'nt for Pumpkin keepin' this place pristine –

BLUE. You keep Pumpkin outta yo' mouth, nigger.

P-SAM. This ain't just your club. This club belong to everybody who done had a piece in keepin' it alive. And you damn straight you owe us, nigger. You owe every moe in Black Bottom! We the backbone of this place. And if you ain't had us, you ain't had nothin' but bricks.

BLUE. You can have all that and leave me my bricks. This place Paradise to you but it ain't to me. It ain't nothin' but a soul-stealer. You and all these bloodsuckers comin' 'round – nothin' but a bunch of worthless niggers scrapin' the bottom of the barrel and livin' on pipe dreams. You can die here, nigger. But I ain't.

P-SAM. Worthless?!

BLUE. That's what I said.

P-SAM. I'll show you worthless, motherfucker.

> (**P-SAM** *lunges into* **BLUE**. *They tussle.*)

CORN.	PUMPKIN.
Sam!	Blue!

> (**P-SAM** *and* **BLUE** *are at each other's throats.*)

> (**CORN** *tries to pull them apart and gets knocked back.*)

> (**SILVER** *enters and jumps back with a start as the men come charging her way.*)

> (*Finally* **P-SAM** *pins* **BLUE** *and starts choking him.*)

(**PUMPKIN** *runs out of the room.*)

(**CORN** *rushes over to* **P-SAM**. **BLUE** *struggles.*)

CORN. Sam, no! Let him go, Sam. Let him go.

P-SAM. I should kill you, you sellout motherfucker!

CORN. No, Sam. Let him go.

(**CORN** *tries to pull* **P-SAM** *off of* **BLUE**. **BLUE** *gasps and catches his breath.* **CORN** *grabs* **P-SAM**.)

P-SAM. Get off me, Corn! Let me go!

(*Finally* **CORN** *releases* **P-SAM**, *who tries to catch his breath.* **BLUE** *rises quickly and charges over to* **P-SAM**, *grabbing him from behind in a headlock.*)

(**BLUE** *pulls out a knife.*)

CORN. Blue...

(**P-SAM** *struggles in* **BLUE***'s grip.*)

BLUE. Who you gonna kill, nigger?

CORN. Blue, don't...

(**SILVER** *moves behind the bar and searches for some kind of weapon.*)

BLUE. You wanna kill me, nigger? Hunh? Then do it. Do it right now.

(**P-SAM** *struggles in* **BLUE***'s grip with urgency, gasping.*)

(**PUMPKIN** *runs onstage with the revolver in her hand.*)

(*Gunshot.*)

(*Everyone halts.* **P-SAM** *falls from* **BLUE***'s clutch, alive and gasping.*)

(**PUMPKIN** *holds her hand high in the air. The gun smokes.*)

(Everyone stares at her, stunned.)

PUMPKIN. Next one won't be no warning.

*(**CORN** moves toward **PUMPKIN**, slowly.)*

CORN. Pumpkin...gimme that now...gimme that gun...

*(**PUMPKIN** aims the gun at **BLUE**.)*

PUMPKIN. The devil is in you. I can... I can see it now. I see it.

*(**BLUE** stares at **PUMPKIN** like she's a stranger. A betrayer.)*

CORN. Come now, Pumpkin. Go'on gimme that...

PUMPKIN. *(To **SILVER**.)* I want it to stop.

SILVER. *(Cautiously.)* Okay...

PUMPKIN. All the ailin', you hear me? Every last part of it. I want it to stop.

CORN. It's gonna stop, Pumpkin. We all gonna be okay, now. Just let it be...

*(**CORN** reaches out to **PUMPKIN**. She turns the gun on him.)*

PUMPKIN. No!

CORN. Okay. It's okay, Pumpkin. Gimme that gun...

PUMPKIN. I say no! No more.

*(**PUMPKIN** waves the gun from **CORN** to **BLUE**.)*

I'm not leaving. Every part of this place is who I am. It's killin' you but it's keepin' the rest of us alive. I can't let you take me from here, Blue. You just ain't right. I see now. You ain't never gonna be. You already gone.

CORN. Blue, grab your trumpet.

BLUE. Say what?

CORN. Go on that stage. Play your axe. Get ready for tonight.

BLUE. I ain't –

CORN. You do it now, Blue. That's what we need right now. We need a soothin'. Ain't that right, Pumpkin?

BLUE. Corn, you talkin' crazy.

CORN. Do it, Blue. This is the moment. You got to play for your soul now.

> (**BLUE** *looks at* **CORN**. *Then at* **PUMPKIN**, *who keeps the gun aimed straight.*)

Play like you gonna kill all them demons and open up the gates of heaven in your song. Play your axe.

> (**BLUE** *slowly walks to the stage, questioning each step, unsure whether to follow...but something in him does.* **PUMPKIN** *follows his path with the gun. Hands steady.*)

> (**BLUE** *reaches out for his horn.*)

> (*He plays a note. Stops.*)

BLUE. I'm losing it.

CORN. Nah, you ain't. I see it in your eyes, Blue. This the moment. It's gon' come right and perfect. You just got to keep playin'. Love Supreme.

> (**BLUE** *considers. He tries again. Begins a tune.*)

> (*Soft at first, then increasingly beautiful.*)

> (*The trumpet sings.*)

> (*Then suddenly, a white light washes over* **BLUE** *as he plays.*)

> (*Everyone stares at* **BLUE**, *transfixed and mesmerized.*)

> (**PUMPKIN** *is caught in the music. It is her prayer. She lowers the gun slowly, hypnotized.*)

> (**BLUE** *plays a long-lasting note. It's the most beautiful note we've ever heard.*)

(Then finally, he stops. He is sweating. He is crying. His body shaking with pain and guilt and sorrow.)

(The white light over him becomes even brighter.)

*(**CORN** nears **PUMPKIN**, eyeing her lowered arm and gun in hand.)*

See, Blue? You found it. That moment of perfect harmony. We your witnesses. Seen it all. And it's time for the madness to stop now. End on a good note.

*(**BLUE** wipes his tears. He smiles peacefully.)*

Ain't that right, Pumpkin?

*(**CORN** looks at **PUMPKIN**. He nods at her knowingly. He steps aside from her. **PUMPKIN** is clear, confident, resolved.)*

PUMPKIN. That's right. For everybody. No more hurtin'.

*(**PUMPKIN** raises the gun at **BLUE**.)*

(Gunshot.)

(Blackout.)

End of Play